Two Paras of Everyday Wisdom

Perspectives & Reflections

Dr. Sandeep Atre

INDIA · SINGAPORE · MALAYSIA

ISBN 979-8-88883-670-5

INTRODUCTION

"It can't solve your problems, but it will help you get sorted" – If I were to choose a one-liner for this book, it would be this one.

Yes, this book doesn't come with a promise to change your life. It only comes with a premise to help you gain perspective. And that I guess is a pretty good contribution that a book can make. So, rather than giving you a "knowhow", it will help you "know" greater so that you can choose your "how" better. Often, that's all it takes – an angle we missed, a point of view we ignored, a standpoint we didn't understand, or a perception we didn't reconsider. You will be surprised how much just a little can change.

This book has grown organically. I have been writing a blog for years now, and many people in my orbit follow it affectionately. They relate to the blog as the posts are about matters related to everyday issues like self, relationships, and work. Interestingly, they also find the format as appealing as the content. Yes, as I evolved as a writer, so did my posts' format – theme-lines, two paragraphs, and culminating lines. Well, people have found this combination of "content and format" quite suited to their reading preferences.

This book is a collection of selected posts from my blog – ones which people, over the years, have identified most with and got most benefited by. I hope you will also find value in them…

Wishing you "happy reading" of the **two paras of everyday wisdom**.

Dr. Sandeep Atre

1

**Happiness comes when you bring
all the aspects of your life in harmony.**

* * *

You can't chase happiness. In fact the more you chase it the farther it goes away. Yes, achievement can be strived for, joy can be arranged or thrill can be sponsored. But happiness? Nah! You can't make it happen, you have to let it happen. It's an offshoot.

It's an effect that manifests in a life which has all its constituting elements in sync with each other, resonating effortlessly. Yes, it's about balance. It is about a place for everything and everything at its place. It's that fine-tuning that is struck with clarity and will power.

* * *

**It's not about pace and magnitude,
it's about the ratios and proportions.**

2

Good listeners listen not only to the other person,
but also to themselves.

* * *

In a world where people find it hard to really listen to the other person, understandably a major part of listening that most people are unaware of or negligent towards is listening to themselves during a conversation. However, when incorporated, that's what makes listening complete and significant.

Yes, in a conversation, listen to yourself as well – What did you say? Was it what you really wanted to say? Did it make sense? Was it relevant? Was it logical? Was it apt? How will the other person perceive it? How will it affect them? How will it change course of the conversation? Why did you say it?

* * *

It's not for nothing that the ears closest to
your mouth are your own.

3

We are not gonna be around forever, so how about choosing what you "pay attention to" in life.

* * *

Not all of us are lucky to choose our experiences, and those of us who can cannot do it all the time. So whenever you have privilege of a choice, you should exercise that choice to choose what gives you *'maximum happiness'* without depriving someone else of theirs.

When you do so, some of them will call you choosy, some of them aloof, and then some others will mock you for 'living in a bubble'. Well, let them say it. That's their choice. You just stay true to what you have chosen and give it your *100% attention*. In the process, you will realize that...

* * *

Life is not what happens to you. It is what you pay attention to.

4

**The ability to diffuse tension is also a
required part of a leader's skill-set.**

❋ ❋ ❋

Whether at workplace or at homes, all is not well always. There are difficult moments and tense phases. Well, in such situations, most people are simply clueless. They don't know what to do and thus stay inert, just like that flowerpot in the corner – waiting to be picked up, both in matter and in spirit.

But a leader cannot leave things to chance or wait inertly. While they must be patient and give ample time for tension to run its due course of time, it is important for them to also know when to pitch in and lift the room back to normalcy. And it's not some inborn talent. Like any other skill…

❋ ❋ ❋

**It starts with awareness, goes via knowledge
and culminates on practice.**

5

**People who perform averagely yet consistently
are important equally.**

* * *

Everyone hails the superstars in the team – the movers and shakers. And honestly, they deserve it as well, because excellence is not easy, as it takes a lot out of you. But due to this exhausting burden of performing in the top gear, these superstars are prone to ups and downs – an awkward inconsistency.

Then there are plain workers – the hoovers and bakers. There is nothing special about them. They have neither an eye for detail nor a heart for creation, and only churn out average stuff. But you know what! By doing their job with an optimum quality but day in day out, they keep ship steady and wolves at bay.

* * *

**Well, for what they secure and procure,
they deserve respect for sure.**

6

For growing kids, parents are the opposing force they discover and build their strength through.

* * *

Visualize a wrestler doing pushups. What is he doing? He is actually pushing the floor, and in the process discovering as well as building their strength. Now imagine that the floor crumbles. What will happen then? Or for that matter, imagine if the floor starts pushing the wrestler back. What will happen now?

Similar is the case of parenting a teenager. Teenagers will always push their parents – disagree, argue, hurt, challenge, rebel; and that too to the extent that the parents will begin to feel disrespected and unwanted. As a result, some of them feel hopeless, some retaliate, and some of them simply walk out.

* * *

But hey! Don't you leave Dads and Moms! You are the floor. Stay there. Work is in progress...

7

**Don't trick yourself into believing that you are someone special
who is ignored by the world. It's a trap.**

✿ ✿ ✿

"You are special" is a good thought, but it shouldn't become an excuse
for an inflated sense of self. After all, if everyone is unique, then
there is no way to tell who is special. Thus, while we must maintain a
healthy self-image with high esteem, we shouldn't do a con job to our
own mind.

Well, most of us have an unduly unfair assessment of our abilities
(too high or too low). To this typical creator's bias, add some ego-
pumping books or videos, and you have a perfect recipe for self-
obsession. And then, if you aren't acknowledged enough by enough
of them, world seems to be an unfair place.

✿ ✿ ✿

**You are not special. You are unique.
And that should suffice.**

8

**We don't live in bungalows, duplexes or flats.
We live in our minds.**

* * *

Yes, that's our permanent residence. And there are no constraints of square-feet there. It's a vast space with unlimited area. And you know what! No matter how well-organized your rooms, balconies, garages and verandas are, life is good only when things are *sorted* there – in your mind.

And that's where we keep things messy – regrets piling up in one corner, expectations stuffed in a closet, secrets under the carpet, worries littered everywhere, comparisons spilt on the table, complexes leaking from an old bottle, and grudges stinking in a box.

* * *

Mind it! For this real home of yours, you can't outsource housekeeping. You got to do it yourself.

9

**Sometimes, people secretly start
enjoying their problems.**

* * *

They begin to selectively talk to people who feed their sense of problem by discussing in detailed and even exaggerated ways, and avoid those who refuse to collaborate in their masochistic game and rather try to bring their focus away from problem and towards a solution mindset. But why do they do so?

Well, it all starts with a genuine craving for empathy – they just want to be heard and understood. But gradually, they begin to prefer comfortable inertia of mere discussing over discomforting proposition of doing something about it. Add to it the attention they are getting, and you've got them hooked.

* * *

**Alas! It's akin to itching for pleasure,
and ending up with a wound.**

10

When you will see life for long enough, you will find that there are no friends and foes…there is always a phase that comes and goes.

* * *

Yes, when you will see life for long enough, you will stop thinking in terms of types and slots. You won't categorize people anymore. You will see the best of your friends leaving you in lurch, and the worst of your adversaries defending you. You will see absolute strangers helping you out of nowhere, and your own people looking at your plight as a bystander.

You will see indifference in the eyes of those for whom you slog day in day out, and you will see kindness in eyes that you thought were made of stone. Well, that's life – at its ironical, comical, whimsical and lyrical best. When you will see life for long enough, you will find that it is a puzzle that no one knows…

* * *

…there is just a stream of experiences that stutters and flows.

11

**The most unfortunate thing in life is to become
victim of our own imagination.**

❋ ❋ ❋

As a person, sometimes we choose an underlying theme for our
'life and self'. It comes in many forms – Misunderstood Manisha…
Overburdened Ojas… Neglected Nitin… Dominated Daljeet…
Adjusting Arjun… Ignored Ishaan… Deprived-of Dominick…
Misinterpreted Mehrunisa etc.

After some time, this theme no more remains an inference of an
experience but becomes the premise to see them through. Yes, we
begin to reinforce the theme either by focusing only on experiences
that align with the theme or by interpreting those experiences in the
light of the theme.

❋ ❋ ❋

**And that's when…we begin to fall prey
to our own imagination.**

12

**Nothing that you will build will
stay forever, so relax.**

❋ ❋ ❋

I am a sucker for greatness, and believe me, there is no better sight in the world than to see someone chasing it. It is pure unadulterated delight to see an aspiring soul… driven by razor-sharp focus… running full throttle and defying the laws postulated by the no-shows. Aha! The stuff the legends are made of.

Yet, I am an equal believer in respect for impermanence and acceptance of transience, and firmly hold that "You can't let fire in the belly burn the belly". So it's important to love the chase and still not get obsessed with it. The reason is simple – every chase is merely a blink in the eternal flow of limitlessness.

❋ ❋ ❋

**So, give your best…storm the chase,
and yet…do not forget to have fun.**

13

Professional repute gets built, not with a showman's swag, but with a surgeon's solidity.

* * *

Some people still believe in fake it until you make it. They still reckon they can weave the magic with their persona and mannerisms to enter the halls of fame. They still assume that sophistication and style can compensate for lack of substance and sincerity. Problem is – they confuse popularity for repute.

With showmanship or chicanery, you can at best gain popularity. However, reputation is an altogether different virtue. You got to have what it takes. Otherwise you turn out to be a shooting star with no luck for itself. After all, it's not for nothing that they say – "Form is temporary but class is permanent".

* * *

So work for real, or else, you will be damned to live in a constant fear of being found out.

14

The problem with spotlight is that it often takes away your attention from what brought you into it.

* * *

You start to do something for the love of it. Actually that's why you do it well. But now when you do it well, you are spotted. And then come the perks – the recognition, benefits and repute. And gradually, your love shifts from "what you are doing" to "what you are getting". That's the first nail…

Moreover, you now get addicted to being liked. So you care less about what you feel about your work and get more conscious about what others say about your work. Then this desire to 'look good' leads to wearing of masks that don't feel good but help you sustain a persona. That's the second nail…

* * *

And above all, another problem with spotlight is that it forces you to hide your dark spots behind a makeup.

15

At times, there is nothing wrong with the other person. It's just that you outgrow a relationship.

* * *

When you enter a relationship, you do so in a particular set of coordinates – that of age, circumstances, priorities, maturity level etc. The other person looks a perfect-fit on criteria or notions you have at that time. So you enter with a promise to stay forever, and no plan to ever exit. But you forget to factor-in one thing – change. Yup, both of you change with time.

However, as luck would have it, you two change differently. Yes, axis is same but curves are different. And that's when you find it difficult to connect to the same person. Of course, you don't leave it there. You understand and wait…reason and explain to yourself. But you know what; right or wrong, the fact is that you've outgrown the relationship. And it's time for two of you to…

* * *

**Sit, discuss, rework, and
if required…decide.**

16

There comes a point in life when you decide that now you won't do anything you don't believe in.

❋ ❋ ❋

Many times in the name of desperation, some times in the name of maturity, at times in the name of accommodating, and at other times in the name of stability, most of us keep doing either the things that we don't feel convinced about or in ways that we don't have complete conviction in.

And then, one day, suddenly you discover that you have had enough. At once, all reasons of holding back are no more as appealing or appalling, and force within is too strong for the rationalization to bear. In such moments, don't just jump off the bus. Wait for storm to pass, and then…

❋ ❋ ❋

…crosscheck whether you are equally clear about "what you believe in".

17

**Discipline is not about dullness,
it is about balance.**

* * *

Most people mistakenly associate "being disciplined" with "being dull or mechanical". They think that discipline is about surrendering life to routines and schedules and making it a dry experience devoid of energy, joy or creativity. They think it is about boredom, when in fact, it is the… exact opposite.

Discipline is not only about "everything on time" but also about "time for everything". It is about taking out time for "Me-time and We-time" as religiously as for work or studying. It is about the all-important moderation which makes your happiness more sustainable and creativity more consistent.

* * *

**Embrace 'discipline' with joy and
witness the difference.**

18

**Success isn't about doing one thing greater,
but doing many things little better.**

* * *

In a world where people are hell-bent on attaching 'success' with words like 'secret', 'mantra' or 'code', it looks clichéd to talk about success as a process of incremental progression. However, that's precisely what it is. Except some cases of serendipity, "process" still remains the norm in every domain.

So don't try to find, search or get success, rather "work towards" it. It's a journey which is best relished when taken. Don't make it look like an event that happens, it is a momentum that builds bit by bit, and finally culminates into an event – an event which is actually outcome of a process.

* * *

**So, the final word on success is –
read the whole book to reach this final word.**

19

Final fun lies in facing your fears.

* * *

Yup! There's fun in lazing around with the TV on, or in dancing
to the similar beats with the rehearsed (and still weird) moves,
or listening to the so-called favorite song that invokes the same
memories, or cracking the stale jokes about mundane topics on same
pals who retort the same way.

But believe me there is fun also in feeling your heart beating right up
to your ears with a stereophonic sound-effect as "one more time" you
approach your emotional nemesis – the one that you dread, run away
from, feel nervous about, avoid at all costs, get stuck in, and could
never look beyond.

* * *

Yup! That's fun – the fundamental fun.

20

**If your closest people don't join you in your battles then
don't hold it against them.**

* * *

I mean they didn't sign up for standing by your side for everything.
Did you ask them before making that move against the odds? Did you
consult them before that stupid rush of blood you surrendered to?
Did you pay heed to their words when you decided to not toe
the line?

Well, honestly, if it was optional for you to include them in your
choices, it is always optional for them to shoulder the weight of the
consequences of your actions. So now stop blaming them for leaving
you alone. They are as much entitled to make their choices as
you were.

* * *

**And above all…why do you forget that they also have
their own battles that you are not aware of.**

21

**The best gift you can give to your mother is
to let her be a woman as well.**

＊ ＊ ＊

She did not realize when she began being more of a mother and less of a woman. Now, it's up to you to not let her become a sentimentally-blackmailed, overburdened, emotionally-dependent, eternally-worried sacrificial being, who works on all seven days from dawn to dusk and still feels the guilt of not doing enough. It's up to you now to save her from the tag of 'Being next to God'.

Let her stay human. Let her feel light. Let her laze around, have fun, enjoy her space, get romantic, be ambitious, pamper herself, spoil her indulgences or simply be herself. Go and tell her "I love you a lot Mom, but I also love dad, granny and grandpa. You are not the ONE. And I will also not hog your spotlight anymore. I'll be OK. Focus on yourself, and elsewhere. Breathe easy mom".

＊ ＊ ＊

**After all it shouldn't be Happy "Mother's Day"
but "Happy Mother's" Day.**

22

**When you grow old, very old,
make sure you have a story to tell.**

* * *

A story that has emotions of a drama, softness of a romcom, hopes of a mystery, twists of a thriller, giggles of a spoof, possibilities of a fantasy, search of a sci-fi, spikes of an action, experiments of an adventure, message of a social, and flow of a saga.

A story about someone who saw and felt, who walked and fell, who learnt and grew, who hugged and held, who sobbed and sang, who loved and lost, who risked and frisked, who tried and failed, who earned and gave, and then who forgot and forgave.

* * *

**When you grow old, very old,
make sure you are a story to tell.**

23

**Monks are all in the mountains, we are
just lesser mortals at work.**

* * *

There is no book or meditation-technique that makes you absolutely neutral. I mean, I have never met a person who doesn't get hurt when they fall. Yes, when things go wrong, it is natural to feel bad… and may be a bit bitter. It's a knee-jerk reaction which only proves that there is a sensation.

Problem starts when you begin to attach negative outcomes with your self-esteem… when you begin to take criticism as a personal assault…when you see a roadblock as the end of the road for you… when you see booing as a hint for you to retire… or when you take an episode as writing on the wall.

* * *

**That's when you should rush to the mountain;
not to be a monk, but to take a break.**

24

**Don't blame people for not moving on.
It takes time.**

❋ ❋ ❋

When your words or deeds hurt someone or cause harm, you cannot expect that a 'sorry' should mend it immediately. After all, your "sorry" came either out of guilt that you felt at your convenience or introspection that you did at your own pace.

Moreover, you can't estimate the magnitude of loss or the intensity of resultant pain, as it is "their" loss. So, it's unfair of you to expect that the other person should shed it off and look ahead just like that. They will take time to come to that point.

❋ ❋ ❋

**You got to understand that your 'Sorry'
cannot bring back what they lost.**

25

**Most of us figure out how to live our life
after most of it is gone.**

❋ ❋ ❋

Isn't it strange and unfair as well! Well, even if it is, believe me, that's the way it turns out for most of us. After all the costly mistakes and avoidable losses, one day, the "way to be" suddenly dawns upon you. And you wonder why, all this while, you couldn't see it.

But you know what! It's not for nothing that they call life a journey… an exploration. Yes, agreed, that with some more patience and maturity, you could have learnt it a less harder way, but isn't it good that at least now you know how to do it a bit better…live a little wiser.

❋ ❋ ❋

**So why not start afresh! From here, now,
and make the best of…the rest of it.**

26

The most annoying and corrosive trait
a person can have is… moodiness.

❄ ❄ ❄

Some people are perpetual pendulums. They would be fine, and then suddenly you would find them sulky or grumpy. One moment they are talking normally and they would abruptly turn indifferent or distant. Phew! You can never predict what's coming your way.

They keep you guessing, and through it, hijack attention and eat away a major chunk of your mental energy. To have them around is like having something simmering on brain's backburner – you can never ignore it. It's so draining and exhausting to deal with them.

❄ ❄ ❄

So, stay closer to emotional "arithmetic mean",
else…"So mean of you".

27

**Don't get confused between
doing something good and something big.**

❋ ❋ ❋

Not every venture needs to be scaled up. Not every talent needs to be showcased to the whole world. Not every music piece needs to be made viral. Not every initiative needs to feature in newspapers. Not every pursuit needs to be commercialized. Yup! It's ok if some entities stay in their orbit and keep working on their own terms. After all, that's also "success" in one way.

Don't get me wrong. If outreach happens, that's great. But it shouldn't be an obvious progression dictating every entity's life-cycle, or else the "good" and "big" get jumbled. Of course, in some cases, good can be made big as well; but in some cases, the texture of the work or fabric of the entity is such that effort to make it big squeezes the good out of it. And then, it goes nowhere.

❋ ❋ ❋

**There are alternative definitions of success.
"Making it big" isn't the only one.**

28

**Greats gravitate more towards
the 'grill' than the 'thrill'.**

* * *

Oh that ordinary being… who craves the highs and shuns the lows… who wants the claps and avoids boos… who chooses the shining spotlight over the solitary lamp on a desk defying the darkness of the sleepy long nights. Oh that ordinary being… who guarantees ordinariness for himself every very day.

Oh that legend in the making… who craves the fulfillment of failing forward over an easy success on offer… who is obsessed with tiny details and not with the façade that looks beautiful… who focuses on mundane habits rather than marvelous slogans. Oh that legend in the making… who builds greatness day by day.

* * *

**Oh those greats… who put extraordinary efforts
to overcome their ordinariness!**

29

**It's always your relationship with your closest people
that defines the quality of your life.**

* * *

In the era of networking, most people seldom pause to see when networking is not working for them. In the race to maximize the 'number' of people they can reach, they fail to see that the "extent" of their reach to people begins to decline.

And then starts an unfortunate contradiction. They have many people connected to them through virtual networks and numerous associations, but they lack the depth of connection, especially with people who they actually spend their most time with.

* * *

It is this mismatch between their 'public persona' and 'private persona' that slowly corrodes the quality of life.

30

**"I succeeded, I failed, but most importantly…
I carried on".**

* * *

On any day if you can say aforesaid words to yourself, you are home.
Yes, that's precisely what life is about – carrying on. It is important to
take failure in your stride, brush your success away, and carry on…
on the path that aligns with your deepest convictions and
dearest aspirations.

And do so, not to get applause or prove your grit, but because that's
the best way to be. After all, life is not a theater where you always
crave for an audience. It is a journey to be taken, sometimes with
companions, sometimes alone. And in the end, that's what gets
you home.

* * *

**So carry on… and let the light within take you to…
where you truly belong.**

31

**While you should not compromise,
it is still important to learn to adjust.**

❋ ❋ ❋

There is a difference between compromise and adjustment. When you sacrifice your convictions then it is called compromise, but when you sacrifice your convenience then it is called adjustment. That's why, while one should ideally not compromise, one should still be willing to adjust.

However, that isn't what's going on around. Whether at work, at home, or in relationships, today most people do not even want to adjust. They are rigid and frigid. They do not even entertain the thought of accommodating, and see it as being weak, looking meek, or losing their identity.

❋ ❋ ❋

**That's why now we have a lot of cool people
struggling with…coldness in life.**

32

**I don't know about power; but
with love surely comes… great responsibility.**

* * *

Every relationship takes its share of time and energy. You can't just plug-in and plug-out and hope it to be self-sustaining. Form may vary, but every relation demands its due share of investment and commands its lock-in period.

This is the reason why most relationships lose steam quickly. As, in the beginning, it seems that it is all about emotions. However, people later realize that it is also about expectations, obligations, clarifications, and adaptations.

* * *

**You know what! Chasing is fun; but
when it ends…the relationship begins.**

33

**Decide what are you going to be –
a worrier or a warrior?**

* * *

Worriers are inert. They sit and imagine scenarios, and then use the pessimistic possibilities of those imagined scenarios to further make themselves more inert. This way they are able to push away any pursuit of action, and avoid discomfort and toil they will have to incur.

Warriors are movers. Although they are equally mindful of pessimistic possibilities, they don't let those thoughts eclipse their effort or hijack their actions. They use those thoughts to further propel the apt navigation of their actions, while accepting that they may still fall or fail.

* * *

**Decide what you are going to be…
as that'll decide the rest.**

34

**In life, everyone is suffering in
their own unique way.**

❊ ❊ ❊

Just because you don't see someone facing the most obvious or mundane problems of life doesn't mean that everything is fine with that person. Know someone a little more or listen for a little longer and you will realize that everyone has a wound to heal and a pain to bear.

And you cannot see wounds and pain comparatively. You can't assess them in connection to others you have seen or where all you have been. You got to see every wound standalone and relate to its pain in reference to a person's unique context, sensitivity and threshold.

❊ ❊ ❊

**Respect people's sufferings
– they come in all shapes and sizes.**

35

**Strong men don't need to raise the volume
of their voice to exercise influence.**

* * *

For strong men, the weight of their words is enough to get their point across and establish their stand clearly. They don't use sarcasm to pinch, satire to poke, taunts to get even, swearwords to hurt, arrogance to generate awe, or backbiting to release grudges.

They look into eye when they talk and listen. They own their opinions, but are courageous enough to change them when exceptions outnumber evidences. They customize the manner but never the matter. They don't disown their choices, but don't defend them needlessly.

* * *

**Where are they? The strong men, who are
manly enough to... not have to flaunt their manliness.**

36

**Most of us prefer to intellectualize a concept
than to simply put it into practice.**

❋ ❋ ❋

Actually, it is convenient to be a thinker. It doesn't take much –
permutations of some good ideas… combinations of some nice words
and here it is – the perfect recipe for reputation. Of course there
is a lot of mental gymnastics involved to make it sound and seem
slightly (yup, even a shade slightly will do) different from all the ideas
floating all over the digital space.

On the other hand, putting a concept into practice is cumbersome.
You have to rise beyond the abstract vanity of knowing something
and get down to the consuming process of "doing" something. Yup,
there are no phrases to hide behind and no idioms coming to your
rescue. You got to roll up your sleeves, pull up your socks, and get
your hands dirty in the pursuit of change.

❋ ❋ ❋

**… And that, I tell you, is soooooo hard;
or else… why would I be thinking all this.**

37

**It is difficult to deal with people
who are not bad but are difficult.**

* * *

There are some people in your life who don't quite qualify as bad –
because they don't shout, they don't use abusive language, they don't
plot against you, they don't talk behind your back, they don't cheat
you, or for that matter they don't even wish you any evil.

But they are very difficult – they are rigid, they are cold, they are
distant, they get on to your nerves, they can be slightly mean, they
can overlook your presence, they stonewall in conversations, they
don't cooperate, they are not willing to change, they are self-centered.
And what's more painful is that, in dealing with second type
of people...

* * *

**...you often risk becoming
one of the first type.**

38

**Most of us fail twice – first when we fail, and then
when we fail to utilize failure.**

❃ ❃ ❃

Failure can have immense utility, but most of us are so bogged down by the futility surrounding it that we simply fail to see the utility. Of course, prominently, failure introduces us to our shortcomings and flaws, which can then help us include the cycle of introspection and retrospection in our work ethic.

But there is more to it – It can relieve us of the excruciating expectation of always being the best, it can give us the lightness of being imperfect, it can give us opportunity to rationalize our self-image, it can help us go back to a learner's mindset, and it can let us stretch…yawn…and smile at others around us.

❃ ❃ ❃

**Yup! When you don't let failure break you,
then it goes on to make you.**

39

**In life, most people only address those questions
whose answers they can bear.**

✻ ✻ ✻

Most people avoid big questions of life and keep themselves busy with small ones. And they do so not because they can't find answers of big questions, but because they are not ready for their answers. This way, they are able to get through another day without much fuss, and save themselves from a discomforting reality-check.

It is more of a plea than a ploy – to sustain a pace of life they find solace in. It is more of a shield they hold to hide themselves from the mirror that stands staring at them. Yes, it is a defense mechanism that they adopt – to maintain the notion of 'all is well'. However, the question is… "Is really all well"? But you see, most of the people won't answer this question, because…

✻ ✻ ✻

**…this is precisely the kind of question
they want to avoid.**

40

**Life is still the best school.
Experience is still the best teacher.**

* * *

The only difference is that their pedagogy is different. It is not sequential, linear or literal. It is metaphoric, analogical and interpretative. Thus, every incident, every episode, every pain, every humiliation, every smile, every surprise – all of them are lessons in the garb of events.

But they are not declared as lessons and don't look like them. It's your own duty to look at them with an observant eye to derive the learning. However, it is possible only when you look at "what you are going through" as a process to progressively hone you into a better version of yourself. Yes, if you bring an already-full cup, everything spills over.

* * *

**And if you bring a blank slate, you go back
with *words of wisdom written on it*.**

41

**Life is much bigger than
a few events happening in it.**

* * *

Someone hurting you… someone leaving you… someone failing you… all these are events that can be really disturbing when seen *standalone*. But then if you look at the journey you have made till this point, that event is at best yet another in the series of all those events that you have *taken in your stride*.

Yes, you've been there before. And though it feels as if this is worse than all earlier ones, believe me, it felt the same way every time. So, *see this event in backdrop of journey you've had*, and you will marvel at sheer magnitude of life you've witnessed… and the sprawling vastness of all there is *yet to be seen.*

* * *

**So now… come on… flash that toothy smile
and… get back to work.**

42

**Have your definition of success,
beyond the sponsored ideas floating around.**

❋ ❋ ❋

They say "success is a relative term". Yup it sure is; and it is also dynamic. But that's not a problem. The problem is that now it is also becoming a sponsored term. In a world dictated by commercial entities, our lives are constantly nudged by their messages. And that's where things get messy.

These messages create notions of success that suit their creators' intentions best. And here we are, all the time stimulated by this sponsored content, continuously subscribing to these changing notions and thus chasing newer possessions, designations and experiences; only to end up disillusioned.

❋ ❋ ❋

**Yup! Stay true to your definition of success.
It will keep you sane and focused.**

43

**Childhood is beautiful because we believe
that all good things are here to stay.**

❋ ❋ ❋

And then, in the process of growing up, we witness the *transient* nature of everything – we fall in love… then fall out of it, we make friends…then lose them, we buy things…and then forget where we kept them, we get success…then flunk hard, we make principles… and then trade them to make a living, we trust people…then find it nowhere, we dream…and then settle down.

And then, we realize that *nothing is permanent.* Life is just a game of cards. No matter how well you prepare for the game, *the game holds enough cards up its sleeves* to throw you off balance. And you have to live with the deal offered. And most of us are not comfortable with that suspense. Oh! So now, we've got the secret of why childhood actually felt beautiful…

❋ ❋ ❋

**Yes, it was because, in childhood, we looked at the world
not with hope, *but with…* curiosity.**

44

**Never trust when someone says "I am there",
just see whether they were.**

❋ ❋ ❋

No one is good *or* bad, everyone is good *and* bad. Yes, there are times when a person who never talked to you talks for you, one you always found obnoxious rekindles your faith, one who has been your worst critic stands up to defend you, or a certified antagonist risks his own balance to pull you out of a rut.

And out there… standing on the *sidelines* is the sweet-talker you always considered a friend, one who promised he would be there for you forever, one who said she would back you up with her life, one who looked right into your eyes and said *"you would never be alone"*, one who had claimed to stay alongside like a shadow. You can see them all, right down the far end… witnessing your struggle with a blank face.

❋ ❋ ❋

**Of course, this isn't always the case.
But, you know what…"You never know".**

45

**For a successful relationship, it is important
to keep tracking the change.**

❋ ❋ ❋

In any sphere of life, when two persons decide to partner, they decide
on the **basis** of *who they are at that point of time* in life. But *"People
are not events, they are processes"*. So each of them changes with time,
and thus, to keep that partnering going, both got to track the change.

Yes, you change with time and so does the other person – in terms
of situations, priorities, constraints, aspirations, nature. New people
come in life, and with them come new equations. And amidst all this,
what you two share is **bound to** get affected for better or worse. So it's
crucial to keep looking.

❋ ❋ ❋

Well, change is not a matter of choice,
***though** 'accepting it' **still is. And that's** where we mess it up.*

46

**Everyone is in the game. Go, play it wholeheartedly.
Oh! But do remember…it's a game.**

❊ ❊ ❊

If you will see anywhere for long enough, you will see a **game** going on – someone playing his moves and waiting for the other one to make his… someone ready to pounce upon a chance to even the odds of one-upmanship… someone wanting to have a foot in the door to then throw it open… someone calculating how best to use the new kid on the block before he knows he is being played. Yes, everywhere, there is a game going on.

Now, you have **two** options. Either *refuse to play it and incur a cost*, or *agree to play it and pay a price*. In case you opt for the first, stay sane while you see others speeding past you. And if you choose the second, then don't hold yourself back. Wear your masks, remember your lines, and do what the playwright makes you do. However, even in the second case, do not let go of your *authenticity*… do not let the mask become your face… do not let your dialogues dictate your beliefs. Because if that happens, then…

❊ ❊ ❊

**…even if you win the game, you will lose; as then…
the game would have won over you.**

47

For most of us, our life has become a self-perpetuating chain of avoiding consequences.

* * *

Well, you make a wrong action and there is a consequence. And then to avoid that consequence you make another action. And then these two consequences merge and make ground for your next action. Yes, that's about it. You get trapped in that loop of "action – consequence – action" for a very long time.

You know what! One day, you will have to break this loop or else it will consume your life. And the only way to do that is to, for once, not do any action to avoid a consequence. If, in your heart of hearts, you believe that you deserve that consequence then don't avoid it. Accept that consequence.

* * *

Yup! That's the only way to break that chain.
Think about it.

48

**If you are struggling in life then…
struggle properly.**

✳ ✳ ✳

Yes, let it be *pure struggle*. Do not mix *into it* your personal complexes or deeply held regrets or low self-esteem or old grudges or a back-story that has nothing to do with the circumstances at hand. I mean, already you are being beaten, so why give birth to new enemies from your own mental womb?

Nope, you can't afford that luxury right now. So, *just* stick to the fight you are currently a part of, and if at all you are getting crushed in the battle or are being completely outdone, please let it be a suffering coming out of *ongoing onslaught*, and not a *past problem* or a *future foe*.

✳ ✳ ✳

**After all, you got to respect the pain
you are earning from your hard work.**

49

**People who begin their "journey to the top" from bottom
need to learn to bear some fools on the way.**

✳ ✳ ✳

For people starting from the scratch, the passage to success can be
not only difficult but also frustrating. And, in comparison, difficulty
is easier to bear because while you do go through pain, you also feel
good as you are overcoming something challenging, and are growing
in the process.

The relatively tougher part is frustration. On the way, you invariably
meet your share of strong-headed nuts and crackpots who make life
difficult for you. They annoy with their "incompetence concealed by
manipulation" and amaze you with their "stupidity disguised
as chutzpah".

✳ ✳ ✳

**Well, actually they are teachers that teach you
patience, maturity and of course… ability to bear fools.**

50

**Never silence your critics.
They make you think what admirers never can.**

❋ ❋ ❋

It is unfortunate that *we* have begun to become a generation that likes to feel good *all the time*. It's like we have developed this insatiable desire for praise and appreciation. What we don't realize is that this hunger to be liked is becoming a handicap of sorts, not allowing us to evolve. Well, critics help in this regard.

Wait! By *critics*, I don't mean people who comment on your work without understanding it, or take a potshot at you just to get a reaction, or suggest without cognizance of where you are coming from. By critics, I mean people who really know you, your domain, your progression and your pursuit.

❋ ❋ ❋

**When such 'critics' speak, steady yourself…
bow a little… and LISTEN.**

51

Every relationship has its issues. They become problems only when you stop talking about them.

❋ ❋ ❋

It typically goes this way – one of the two gets so frustrated with an issue that he (or she) *gives up*, and becomes quiet. He doesn't raise it anymore, or circumvents when it resurfaces. As a result, the other person feels that it is no more an issue. So both start pretending as if the issue doesn't even exist. And that's when the charade starts hurting…

Yes, though the first person avoids confrontation, it doesn't mean that he doesn't care about it. He still does, but he thinks he is buying peace. However, he is *wrong*, as *silence is not peace*. Just because he doesn't express doesn't mean it doesn't hurt. So, slowly, that effort to hide emotion becomes manipulative and corrosive, leading to gradual distancing of two persons.

❋ ❋ ❋

So TALK; as a relationship devoid of genuine connection is merely an arrangement for others to see.

52

**Patience is not to "not do anything", it is to
allow things to happen once you have done your bit.**

* * *

Often people confuse patience with inaction. Patience is not inaction.
It is to bear the *gestation period* without restlessness and complaining.
But gestation period can only come into picture when you had timely
prepared the farm, sown the seeds, and sprinkled the nourishment.
To now let the land do its bit is called *patience*.

Patience is not unfounded hope, or baseless optimism. It is
not shallow talk replacing the hard yard, or leisurely walk
substituting for *sweating it out*. It isn't useless intellectualizing and
hollow philosophizing. *It* is rooted in pursuit, and grounded in
purposefulness. And only those who had persisted and perspired
earlier have a right to exercise it now.

* * *

**It is interlude in a song, until…
the voice emerges again.**

53

**When you block your schedule with busyness,
there is no time available to accommodate greatness.**

✳ ✳ ✳

One peculiar thing you would typically find with most of us – the middle-class people – is that we try to fill every vacant space in our house with something. It could be anything but the place would get filled somehow. And the reason is simple. We have more aspirations but less space.

Average-performing people tend to do same thing with their time. They fill every gap of their schedule with something. In fact, they feel guilt if they (or others) think they are not doing much. Well, this tendency doesn't let them drop below average because they seldom remain idle. But this also doesn't let them become great…

✳ ✳ ✳

**…because they are addicted to speed,
at the cost of… velocity.**

54

**Taking yourself seriously has
serious consequences.**

❄ ❄ ❄

If you take yourself too seriously then unknowingly you start getting
blackmailed by people into living a life befitting the image *they* have
built for you in *their* own minds. So, now you are just a puppet in
their hands, but interestingly you never feel like that because you also
secretly enjoy the image you are pitted against. And then begins the
most laughable charade…

Yes, you now try to live a life that an "imagined character with your
name and face" lives in people's heads. This charade is so intoxicating
that you don't even pause for a while to question the insanity of it all.
After all, you are not that imagined character. Are you? But it doesn't
even occur to you because of all the importance you get for playing a
second fiddle to your image. Yes! It is this importance that feeds
the game.

❄ ❄ ❄

**So pause, and question the importance of…
this importance.**

55

**When you know your truth,
you have less violence inside.**

* * *

We all are two-faced people – each one of us. Only in our heart of hearts we know who we really are. Our darker side is a well-guarded secret that we meticulously keep, because it's inconvenient to discuss and detail it. But it's right there – coming out of the closet in moments of quiet aloneness.

Well, but that isn't the actual problem. I mean, each of us knows that there is a side to all of us that none of us knows except one of us. The problem is when we disown that side in the name of hiding it. Bad idea. Rather…grope in the dark, and get conversant with what's there. After all, as they say…

* * *

**"It is not the darkness that we are scared of,
it's what the darkness hides".**

56

**When you get offended by every feedback,
people simply give up on you.**

❋ ❋ ❋

Giving feedback is as difficult as receiving it. After all, you put your rapport with the person at stake, risk being perceived negatively, and increase probability of making the other person vengeful and thus inviting a possible loss of repute, reward or even resources. Well, isn't that risking a tad too much?

That's why, if you genuinely want to go up in life, you have to help people trust that they are safe when they give feedback to you. They must trust that you may naturally feel a bit bad about it but have ample reservoir of intellect to process their feedback without an agenda of getting back at them.

❋ ❋ ❋

**And yes! It requires reservoir of
one more thing inside you – self-esteem.**

57

**It's even more *painful* when you don't even know if
the other person is *even connecting to your pain*.**

* * *

It's a strange situation – You are pouring out your most personal
feelings in front of someone. You are talking about your deepest
dilemmas… those terrible traumas… a horrible helplessness… that
repetitive restlessness. And when you lift your chin up and look at the
other person's face, there is nothing on it – just a 'pasted expression'
of some sort.

And suddenly, you get shell-shocked. You feel many things at the
same time – insecurity of trusting too much… embarrassment of
opening up too quickly… regret of letting go too early… fear of being
judged too harshly. You almost feel as if you got naked in front of
an impersonator in the skin of a soul-mate. In those moments, you
realize that…

* * *

**…when you share a part of yourself with someone,
you actually expect a mirror on the other person's face.**

58

**Sometimes the best you can do is to sit on that thought
and let the moment pass.**

✳ ✳ ✳

Yup! A moment comes when the impulse inside you fetches the deeply buried feeling, combines it with the heat of the moment, and is ready to belch it out as piercing words with unusual intensity. Well, what you do in this moment will make or mar… take or leave… redo or undo.

This moment can make a mockery of years of patience, this moment can make a mess which will take years to clear, this moment can relieve the burden that is stifling you from within, this moment can destroy the base on which you are building the life to come. Yup! This one moment.

✳ ✳ ✳

**Wait for a moment! It's just a moment.
Let it pass. Can you?**

59

**No disgrace or glory can define anyone.
It's always something 'in between'.**

* * *

In a way, a negativity bias is natural. However, you can't keep reminding people about their moments of weakness. That's not their true representation. We all have moments when we are at our worst behavior. In fact, it's never far from any of us. Just a bad day or a tough phase, and you discover that the lid can't remain closed anymore and the 'burst bringing out the worst' is inevitable.

At times, you see it building up, and at times you get shocked by the vehemence of it. But that's not you. That's a part of you for sure. Still that's not you. Just the way, 'when everything clicks on a day and you seem invincible' is also not you. That's again a part of you for sure. But still that's not you. You are both of them, and still aren't either of them.

* * *

That's why, when you keep bringing any one extreme as an evidence of *'who you are'* or *'who someone is'* then it is unfair and misleading.

60

**If you love someone, don't wish that
you should be the only source of happiness in that person's life.**

❋ ❋ ❋

In any relationship – and more so in romantic ones – it is natural
to seek attention of the other person. However, a desire to be at
the center of other person's life is sure-shot way of strangling the
relationship beyond recovery. You can't be stubborn about being the
only reason for that person's happiness, because one is too small a
number to base a life on.

The fact is that when two persons become sole reason for each other's
existence, they only sow seeds of future misery and disillusionment.
It's simple. If you want lasting happiness in a relationship, let the
other person receive positive vibes from other people in his or her
life. Otherwise, soon the person will neither be happy nor be yours
for long.

❋ ❋ ❋

**Yes, even if you are possessive,
you can't treat people as possessions.**

61

**You can't go into each mind and correct
your impressions made there.**

❄ ❄ ❄

Each one of us exists as a set of images in people's heads. These images never (yes! never) represent our reality. They are always twisted, tweaked, morphed, imagined, projected or exaggerated. And the best part is that people play with these images to suit their intents and purposes.

As long as this "playing" is on positive side, we all enjoy it. The problem is when people misinterpret you, go on to misrepresent you in the world out there, and other people begin to believe their version of you. And here you are -frustrated and helpless. Well, what to do then?

❄ ❄ ❄

**Nothing. Why fight images and shadows?
Just stay invested in your reality.**

62

**Sometimes it is good to blend with the background
and let someone else receive the applause.**

* * *

To work well with people, more than a bigger brain, one requires a larger heart. It includes sharing credit, forgiving mistakes, ignoring foibles, relinquishing rights, bearing shortchange, and giving up claims. Of course, doing all this isn't easy because most of it doesn't feel good.

That's why, the ultimate test of character is to make sacrifices that are not even spotted, and still smile with contentment because "you" were watching yourself make them in the larger interest. Well, it is not a role for weak-hearted. It requires reasonably high self-esteem and maturity.

* * *

**Yes, sometimes one needs to be strong enough
to let someone else look stronger.**

63

**You can't keep hurting people and
also blame them for being grumpy.**

❋ ❋ ❋

When you exercise your right to behave in a certain manner then you also have to acknowledge that *to let you do so*, there are other people in your life who adjust and sacrifice. Now that adjustment causes its own share of inconvenience and discomfort which those people bear only because they care for you.

However, we all are humans. So that pain will cause those close people to *cringe or shriek* once in a while. And it is very unfair on your part to not allow that occasional outlet just because you don't feel good about it. After all, in lieu of what they have done for you, they at least deserve that leeway.

❋ ❋ ❋

**Respect people's sacrifices. They changed themselves
to let you 'stay the way you are'.**

64

**In life, all targets are
moving targets.**

❋ ❋ ❋

When you are stable inside, you look for instability outside; and when you are unstable inside, you look for stability outside. But the problem comes when, at the outset, you are stable, but somewhere along the way, the instability of outside begins to creep inside. That's when things start to crumble.

Well, no matter how much we admire superhuman traits, fact remains that we all are humans and will revert to our biological and psychological limitations. So, while chasing our target, we must also remind ourselves that all targets are moving targets, and thus we are not going to ever get them every time.

❋ ❋ ❋

**Appreciation of this fact keeps
our sanity intact.**

65

**Holding one person entirely responsible for your misery
is a lie you love to believe.**

* * *

There is always someone who attracts the hatred in you – a boss, a colleague, a partner; a parent, a beloved, a relative. This one person suddenly becomes THE ONE. Everything that goes wrong with you eventually finds the source in this one person, who becomes a bundle of badness.

While this person might have a role to play in your problems, the role is nowhere of the proportion you start to attribute. In fact, often this one person actually incurs cost on behalf of many others –feelings related to whom are cumulatively directed towards this one "representative villain".

* * *

**Distribute your hatred to an extent that
everyone seems a little rascal, but no ONE a scoundrel.**

66

**Difficult times are not for turning depressed,
they are for 'becoming more observant'.**

* * *

There are times when you are on the verge of collapsing, and all you
can think of is 'when'. You can see people walking away, with their
backs towards you. You can hear the murmur in the background
– discussion over your misfortune, with a tone betraying the
effort to show sympathy and revealing the underlying ridicule and
opportunism. However, you are too exhausted to register voices and
too weak to defend your crumbling self.

Well, on such days, when all you want is to surrender to gravity…
that's exactly what you shouldn't do. It's a rare time when life's greatest
lessons are to be learnt. So retain your waning vigilance and see –
see the real colors of people…their true faces…and your place in
their priorities. It's time when all the subplots in your story will get
revealed, and most importantly, you will see your own self with naked
eyes, without the usual make-up.

* * *

**Yes, precisely when tears well up that
your eyes need to be at their sharpest.**

67

**While giving feedback, learn to convey observations
without guessing the reasons.**

* * *

Learn to say "I have observed that…" without adding "And you do
it because…". Yes, people receive feedback as long as they feel they
have an equal standing in the discussion. The moment they sense that
the other person is not giving them enough space on the mat, they
disown the matter.

Then they become defensive, offensive, disinterested or cynical. They
start telling themselves that this is no more a discussion but just an
opportunity for the other person to offload speculations, hypotheses,
selective evidences and preconceived notions to fit the inferences that
serve him well.

* * *

**So have an agreement on observations,
let them tell the reasons, and then discuss further.**

68

**'Move on' in life, but move on
as a wiser person.**

* * *

There will always be people who will hurt you – sometimes unintentionally and at other times 'intentionally'. When they do, it is natural for you to take it to heart for a while. But as time passes, you have a choice of either 'keeping it in heart' or 'letting go'. But I think there is a third alternative. You can forgive the person and not forget the learning(s). Yes, you should store the factual portion of the feeling and let the feeling gradually recede. Easier said than done, but surely worth a try.

After all, it is not the person but the act that hurt you. And don't forget that other people in your life are also perfectly capable of repeating that act. So, update the database and let it work at the backend. Ok Ok! Before you object, I should admit that yes it is difficult to analyze your own hurt by being objective.

* * *

**But then…we have to learn to do so,
to achieve a higher…objective.**

69

**When you are really in love, you have
less complaints with the world.**

* * *

Real love isn't about sad songs of dejected beloveds, jarring dialogues of obsessed lovers, shocking scenes of people breaking things, lonely walks of clueless individuals wearing a hoody, depressed pouters refusing to open the door, oversensitive douchebags dumped in smoke and smell, or cynical loners giving generalized statements about how world works.

Unless it is your first infatuation when hormones do wreak some havoc, any of the above symptoms tells less about the emotion and more about the person. In reality, real love makes you more settled, less restless, more focused, less insecure, more empathetic and less aggressive. And even if it doesn't work out, you accept with pain, part with grace and move on with gratitude.

* * *

**Yes, when you are really in love,
you have more love in you.**

70

**Ambitiousness makes you restless,
progressiveness keeps you inspired.**

❋ ❋ ❋

It is good to get better, richer and stronger. I mean, why not? There is nothing wrong about gaining success, power and fame. Why should we needlessly glorify average existence with anonymity, helplessness, and deprivation? After all, happiness is precisely what all of us are in pursuit of.

Aha! It's this last line that brings it all into perspective. Yes, it all comes down to happiness. And you can't be happy if the fire inside you consumes the fuel that is you. That's why, it is important to grow without desperation or insecurity. That's when it is called progressiveness – the wiser form of ambition.

❋ ❋ ❋

**Yes, it is good to get better, richer,
stronger, and… wiser.**

71

**Neither one good day makes you great nor does
one bad day make you a bygone.**

* * *

Life can change in a day. No doubt it can. Ask a person who won a
lottery or met an accident, or someone who got through an exam or
lost someone. Such extreme events do shape a person and their life
unmistakably. However, in most cases, one day gone off the beat
isn't a decider.

That's why, if you have a terrifically good or a terribly bad day, do
learn to take it in your stride. Don't let it inflate or deflate your self-
concept needlessly. Believe me, it is easier said than done, because our
fragile self-concept is always vulnerable to take such events on their
face value.

* * *

**So, how was your day?
Oh Come on! Add it to life, and…move on.**

72

**If you are going through a difficult phase,
don't extend it by making new mistakes.**

❋ ❋ ❋

Everyone goes through a lean patch occasionally – due to circumstances, mistakes, problems or idiocy of oneself or others. Though its duration is directly proportional to the magnitude of what went wrong, usually, the patch passes on its own, leaving some learning and some bad taste in the mouth.

However, at times, we become overanxious in such a phase – restless to get out of it in a hurry without serving the metaphoric sentence. In that restlessness, we often end up making more errors in judgment, behavior and choices. And that creates another loop of newer consequences to be borne.

❋ ❋ ❋

**Yup! In such a phase… "Stay patient, pay the dues,
and wait for it to get over".**

73

**If you are getting nervous, get nervous
and also keep doing your stuff.**

* * *

It's okay to feel not okay at times – to have that strange uneasy feeling in the stomach when concern gets mixed with sadness; or that queasy heaviness in the head when stress gets mixed with diffidence; or that weird bulkiness in the body when tiredness gets mixed with reluctance.

While these feelings are there for a reason and deserve to be acknowledged, it is important to not wait for them to get over to "get going". You can begin to get on with your journey even with the dwindling morale and jittery steps, without waiting for the perfect timing or right feeling.

* * *

**People who go places are the ones that move,
not in absence of, but in spite of these feelings.**

74

Often the people who come to make a difference in your life aren't packaged to your liking.

❊ ❊ ❊

They come as a rude team-member who makes faces, a skeptic colleague who rips your ideas apart, an unbearable customer who makes you feel miserable, a boss who is straightforward to the extent of being insulting, or a dear one who behaves coldly at your critical juncture.

At times, they have "absolute gems of wisdom" to deliver to you. However they often deliver those gems in combination with a sarcastic tone, a straight-faced manner, some swear words, an argumentative way, a bad mood, foul language, or a below the belt remark.

❊ ❊ ❊

If only we can learn to sometimes ignore the package for what's packaged.

75

**Goodness is not a medal to be worn,
it is a choice to be made.**

* * *

And like any other choice, it comes with a set of consequences –
you are sometimes left vulnerable, sometimes stranded, sometimes
outraged, sometimes taken advantage of, sometimes underestimated,
sometimes finishing last, sometimes manipulated, sometimes taken
granted for, sometimes shortchanged, and sometimes simply ignored.

That's why the only way you can remain good is by developing a
strong deep-rooted self-esteem – an ability to shrug it off with a
smile, to forget the sting, to forgive the rascals, to take the rejection
in your stride, to again take a leap of faith, to ignore the talk behind
the back, to retain the innocence to trust, and to not let humiliation
define your self-worth.

* * *

**Well, it is not an easy road that anyone can tread.
It is only meant for the 'league extraordinaire'.**

76

**Successful people have a responsibility to
prove they are worthy of it.**

❈ ❈ ❈

You would often find successful people doing mediocre work and still managing to get away with it just because they have a 'name' to back it up with. Well, I agree that it is important to respect that that name is built by a series of great works in the past for which the person must have worked pretty hard.

However, once you earn a name, you can either exploit it or prove it right – i.e. either "work harder and create better" or "dish out shallow work and maneuver with presentation". Well, don't forget that there are many people out there who are as worthy of success as you but haven't got it. If you've got it…

❈ ❈ ❈

**Keep proving that you still
deserve it as much.**

77

**There are so many stories that
we are a part of.**

* * *

We all live multiple lives, running parallel to each other. It is as if there are stories spread across us, and we enter one, play our role, and then eject ourselves from that and enter the next one – sometimes by design, sometimes by will, and sometimes by being drawn by other characters.

These stories are of all types – in some, we are valued…in some, we are damned; in some, we are glorified… in some, we are misinterpreted; in some, we play the hero…in some, we play the supporting cast. And the best part is that all these stories are nowhere but…in our own minds.

* * *

**Yup! We are the storyteller. Remember that,
as it will help you stay…sorted.**

78

To continue to do something you like, you have to keep doing an appended one that you don't like.

* * *

For instance, if a kid wants to continue to enjoy sweets right through his childhood, he has to rinse his mouth every time he eats some. However, you would typically see that kids wouldn't do that. Why? Well, because that appended activity is neither pleasurable nor seems urgent.

I call it the "mundane-ness of compensatory mechanism", and it is applicable in all walks of life. Yes, for every glamorous act there would be something tedious to be done to ensure its longevity, and any form of excellence will have its share of dull drudgery to be done to maintain it.

* * *

In other words, for every interesting thing, you have to continue to do an uninteresting one as well.

79

There are no right or wrong decisions. You take a decision, and then prove it right or wrong.

* * *

All decisions are taken on the basis of "analysis of the past", "observation of the present" and "forecasting of the future"; all done in the light of the "possible effects on various stakeholders". The best part is that no matter how well one tries to forecast future, it will always remain a variable in the equation.

When the implementation of decision starts, this variable has to be tracked continuously, as future gradually becomes the present, one moment at a time. This tracking, consequent appraisal of the manner of implementation, and tactical adjustments made as a result, are what help prove a decision right.

* * *

**You can't take a decision and forget it.
You got to live in tandem with it.**

80

**A true friend is the one who can be happy
in your success without getting jealous.**

* * *

"A friend in need is a friend indeed" – For an eon, this line has been the litmus-test for friendship. Well, it shall always hold true now and beyond. However, there is another equally important litmus-test – how do you feel when your friend does better than you? Yup, that's the "moment of truth".

Well, it is natural to compare (and even compete) with even a dear one. But friendship is about countering that first animal instinct with even stronger "vicarious pleasure" born out of affinity. So, ask yourself – do I have some such friends? And more importantly, ask yourself – am I one such friend to someone?

* * *

**Needless to say, we attract
who we are.**

81

**For sensitive people, life can be
quite an arduous journey.**

* * *

Sensitivity always comes with vulnerability – vulnerability to get
affected, hurt, and disillusioned. It's a strange duo. While sensitivity
can make life a beautiful experience experienced at the subtlest of
levels, vulnerability can make it an ugly ordeal to go through both
outside as well as inside.

People who feel profoundly know how tough it can be. What to
do then? Well, there are two ways – first, to insulate yourself from
potential disturbers and live in your space; and second, to raise your
self-esteem to a level where you can deal with disturbers with just a
smile and a shake of head.

* * *

**Yes, sensitivity is a gift – a gift you have to
preserve through sensibility.**

82

**Not everyone who deserves gets. Not everyone
who gets deserves. Get used to it.**

✳ ✳ ✳

There will always be certain randomness about success. You will find
"best of the breed" waiting in the wings and "just about adequate"
ones making it to the rings. It is as if life keeps updating the success-
rules and we only get to guess the new rules by looking at who is
succeeding currently.

And the fun part is that by the time we begin to play by the guessed
new-rules, the rules change again. Then, what's the way out? Well,
try this! Do your own thing and let success come to you on your own
terms. As in any case, if your success comes to you on someone else's
terms then it is…

✳ ✳ ✳

**…someone else's success.
Isn't it?**

83

**In life, sometimes we are
simply solving a wrong question.**

* * *

Why is it always about… just one more room in the house, just one more zero in the pay-cheque, just one more promotion, just one more week of vacation, just one more hour of sleep, just one more degree on the visiting card, just one more chance to prove oneself?

Why can't it be about… just one less dose of desire, just one less round of regret, just one less case of complaint, just one less hounding of harshness, just one less attack of anger, just one less tingling of temptation, just one less episode of envy?

* * *

**I guess latter is a better way
to be more or less 'happy'.**

84

**Never lose yourself in a relation,
and never lose a relation for your 'SELF'.**

❊ ❊ ❊

It's a walk on a tight rope. You can't tilt on either side. If you become too self-centered then relationship suffers, and if you become too sacrificial then you suffer. And most of us err in judgment regarding when to adjust and when to assert. Yes, there is no "Standard Operating Procedure" here.

You have to continuously keep track of what the situation demands – when to let go and when to pull back…when to stay silent and when to confront…when to introspect and when to make someone introspect…when to swallow pride and when to stand for what you stand for.

❊ ❊ ❊

**It's always a balancing act. You just have to
decide how much it is worth it.**

85

Do not be so desperate for something that by the time you get it, you are too emotionally drained to avail it.

* * *

There is a difference between aspiring for something and craving for it. Unfortunately, in an era where we seem to have an insatiable desire for 'motivational' quotes, stories, anecdotes and clips, messages of 'Go for it', 'Now or Never', 'Want it badly enough' are being subtly pushed into adolescent psyche.

While this dose gives a short-term high, it eats into the inner reservoir of the person in the pursuit. The spikes of synthetically risen morale make people see it less as journey and more as 'chase'. And often, by the time you get spotlight, your attention has been away for long enough to be able to make it all count.

* * *

Well, 'drive' is good, but it shouldn't begin to drive you crazy.

86

**Most disagreements in life aren't ideological
but interpretational.**

* * *

When you say something, your words convey a thought that is born in your mind. That thought is a co-creation of some personal variables – your observations, experiences, beliefs and emotions. Now, when your words go out there, people's connection to them is subject to their own unique sets of these personal variables.

So, people's interpretation of your words is always bound to be slightly different from what your words originally meant. Often disagreements arise due to this variation. That's why it's crucial to differentiate whether someone's disagreement is due to difference in opinion or difference in interpretation.

* * *

**Bring this maturity, and you will not
disagree with every disagreement.**

87

**A creator should understand that every
creation has its own destiny.**

❊ ❊ ❊

Whether you conceive a project, start a venture, begin an assignment,
or give birth to a child, it is important to let go at some point of time.
You have to respect that now the creation has an existence beyond
you. It will have its own struggles…its own glory…its own journey.
You are at best a part of it.

I am not talking about disowning it or not giving your best. You got
to do it, that's your duty; after all, it's a part of you. All I am talking
about is to let it breathe, to not possess it so much that the creation
never owns itself and always remains tied by the umbilical. You have
to let it relate to the soil directly.

❊ ❊ ❊

**Remember! What was once in your womb now
belongs to the world. Accept it.**

88

It's important to see life as an assembly line which is working on a product – YOU.

* * *

You may ask why you should be observant and introspective towards life! Well, the reason lies in the basic premise one should have for life. Begin to believe that all experiences you go through, people you come across, incidents that take place, and events that transpire are there for a reason. See a sense of subliminal plot at work, as if a script is unfolding.

You can call it destiny – not in sense of luck or kismet but in sense of "navigation to a destination" (notice the similarity in two words "destiny" and "destination"). What is happening to you is shaping you, and all of it is taking you towards what you are meant to be. They will all add up. Yes, you should see each experience not in terms of what it does for you, but…

* * *

…what it does to you.

89

**When we blame others for our failure, we miss an opportunity
to build the strength of our character.**

❋ ❋ ❋

It's understandable if one loses cool to safeguard life, belongings or
dignity of one's self and loved ones. However, there are times when
we blame others just to let out our aggression or frustration. It serves
a purpose, as "the shortest route to short-term elevation of self-image
is by vilifying someone".

This is not only wrong but also complete waste of an opportunity.
After all, only by owning the failure can one build foundation for
successes to come. We can't deflect responsibility of what happened
and hope to grow as a person. So, rather than dumping our angst, let's
give it a constructive outlet by...

❋ ❋ ❋

**...using it to whet our
wisdom and willow.**

90

**Don't try too hard to impress people. It will take
a toll on your self-esteem.**

❊ ❊ ❊

Well, we all try to impress people – sometimes because we want to
and sometimes because we have to. As 'social animals', it is a natural
tendency born out of requirement of acceptance. And then there are
demands of situations, occupation and other such understandable
reasons for doing so.

However, the problem comes when we try "too hard" to please
or be liked by going out of the way. That's when the things take
pathological proportions, and we begin to experience that restlessness
for grabbing eyeballs for the reasons beyond the ones we wanted to
'get noticed for' in the first place.

❊ ❊ ❊

**Let's impress through what we want to be known for
and not because we want to be …known.**

91

**Good times don't last forever.
So, if you have tide on your side…keep sailing.**

* * *

At times, fortunes change so suddenly that you are not able to
even register what happened. Yes, in a day's time, worlds come
down crashing. It is as if a giant wave comes and takes away with it
everything you had built, leaving the shore so calm and empty as if
nothing was ever there. And you aren't even sad or angry, you are
simply…numb.

That's why it is important to respect the vicissitudes of time, and
live in resonance with it. So, if you are going through a good
phase, don't waste it. Avoid inflated ego, petty battles, bare-chested
bragging, needless reshuffling, indulgent over-thinking, misplaced
ambitiousness or tempting distractions. Simply stay focused and keep
giving your best.

* * *

**Because if the tide will turn, you will realize how you
never heard a giant clock ticking up there.**

92

**Do not get so obsessed with a dream that
it starts affecting your reality.**

❃ ❃ ❃

Ideas can be really seductive. They can cast such a spell over you that
you begin to chase one of them as if your life depends on it. It takes
form of a dream…a vision…or an ideology. However, no matter how
'great' it sounds, it is at best an idea – an abstraction…a conception.

Well, I have no problems if this abstraction motivates you to take
up a journey. But at times, an image of your future-self becomes so
overpowering that you stop enjoying the reflection you see every day
in the mirror. All you care about is that "One day, I will…" image.
And that's when…

❃ ❃ ❃

**…that idea requires a reality-check
– a comeback to sanity.**

93

**Don't pack your schedule so tight that there remains
no scope for an unexpected opportunity.**

✳ ✳ ✳

I know life is a tradeoff…and that you will have to lose something to gain something else…and that a bird in hand is better than two in the bush…and that you can't have it all. Still, I will make my case – let's not pack our schedules with activities just to placate the insecurity of seeming idle.

And I am not talking about "not scheduling" your day. In fact, I have always been a great proponent of productively utilizing every day with planning and self-directedness. What I am questioning is our growing tendency to 'be busy with trivial to look busy all the time'.

✳ ✳ ✳

**After all, you can plan the efforts
but not the opportunities.**

94

**Unresolved past makes your present bear burden of
a ghost that didn't die properly.**

✳ ✳ ✳

Past is past because it has passed, but what will you call a past that
hasn't passed? Yes, there are times when the past doesn't pass, some
part of it remains painfully alive. It lingers on… and keeps entering
your present off and on.

And then, it becomes a constant struggle, to pull your present from
the clutches of past, to rightfully own it. But the past doesn't loosen
its grip. The more you pull, the tighter it holds. You know what! This
tussle won't end until…

✳ ✳ ✳

**…you do something in your present to
give that past a redeemed future.**

95

**Planning to do something cannot be
a substitute for "Doing it".**

* * *

There are a lot of planners out there in the world. They know all that has to be done, in impressive details. They talk with great gusto and complete conviction. Listening to them is a crash course in "how to win friends and influence people", except "they never get down to actually do much".

On the surface, it might seem that they were fooling you, but the fact is that they have been successfully fooling themselves, manipulating their own selves into believing that one day they will do it. As a result, they feel increasingly lesser guilt and greater pleasure in 'talking their plans out'.

* * *

Let's not be one.

96

I shout because I suffer.

❋ ❋ ❋

When I suffered in silence, you thought I was dull and glum. You criticized me for not being communicative. You called me names, and when I didn't react, you again called me names. When I tried to explain, you ignored, smiled with contempt, or just didn't want to understand.

And then…I started shouting. Not because I wanted to intimidate, but because I wanted to be heard. I wanted you to know that I am suffering. But now, you think I have gone mad…that I have lost it… that I am no more reasonable, and hardly mature. Alas…you don't understand that…

❋ ❋ ❋

**…now I shout, not because I have something to gain.
It's actually a shriek out of sheer pain.**

97

**See life as a process of continuous improvement,
not as standalone *failures and achievements*.**

* * *

Do not infer the state of your life after every experience. Neither the good ones make life absolutely good nor do the bad ones make it utterly bad. Experiences have to be seen in a composite manner, assessed in relation to each other.

For this you will have to connect the dots, and you can't connect them by sitting on one of those dots. You got to have a bird's eye view, with entire landscape of your life laid out on a table while you look at it as if it weren't your life but someone else's.

* * *

**And for that objectivity, first you got to
have enough dots on the paper.**

98

**Some people prove their existence by creating
and some by…destroying.**

* * *

All humans have an intrinsic desire to matter – to prove that they
also exist and have an identity. After all, insignificance is such a
humiliating feeling. You feel as if you are just an ant in the universe.
That's why people, in their orbits and in devised ways, ensure that
somehow their presence gets registered.

And two fundamental ways in which they do so is by supporting or
opposing, hailing or criticizing, or let's broadly say – by constructing
or destroying. But while constructing is hard and lengthy, destroying
is easier. That's why you see those who are unable to create almost
becoming…liable to destroy.

* * *

**To Greeks, Eros is God (drive) of creation and Thanatos
of destruction. Alas! They coexist in us.**

99

Work was always supposed to be only a part of life.
Let's reassess the space it is occupying in our heads.

* * *

My point isn't about the time that work is occupying, it is about the space in the head. Yup, that's where the pain-point for us – the modern humans – is. When it comes to life, work should be EQUALLY important, not the MOST. It is not what life should revolve around – mentally or emotionally.

Sample this - Now we call our holidays 'getaways'. Why a 'get-away' from work, why can't we call it a "get-towards" something. Whatever it is – art, nature, family, or life in general – that is what is supposed to be in focus, not what we are getting away from. Well, such rephrasing requires serious reassessment.

* * *

Yes, there is so much more to life.
If only… we can 'work it out'.

100

**It's amazing how you connect to some people so effortlessly,
as if a part of you always knew them.**

* * *

With some people, conversation simply flows…there is no need to think of the next thread. Movement of current thought to next and then to the previous and then to other in connection to all the earlier ones is so seamless that you hardly realize it is happening.

It's almost like a trapeze artist happily flowing from one swing to another. There is a rhythmic pattern of words, smiles, touches, chuckles. There is even an intuitive understanding of when to listen and when to speak…when is a pause a pause and when is it a passing of baton. And all this happens because…

* * *

**…there is 'total immersion and
undivided attention'.**

101

**Nothing hurts one more than an indifferent God
and an uninterested parent.**

* * *

Few things have a deeper impact on an individual than how they
are parented. While you can script your life as you grow up, your
emotional vocabulary – for better or worse – gets installed right at the
outset. Yes, you learn to make sense of the world by engaging with the
ones who introduce you to it.

And what if they are there but not there for you – too busy with other
things, too invested elsewhere, too distracted by their own issues, too
forgetful to pay attention, or too negligent to navigate? Well, then
what happens is that nothing happens. The result is a person with
voice but no vocabulary.

* * *

**It's like having a God who was making you
and lost interest in the middle of it.**

102

**Sometimes, the road ahead is so stuck, that
to move ahead, you have to move out.**

* * *

It's never easy to walk away. It takes far too much out of you to bear with a grin or put up a brave front. While you feel pain of leaving it behind, you also feel guilt of letting a part of yourself down. But then, sometimes, that's the only way left to stay afloat.

It is not easy, was never meant to be. So be ready for some leftover pain never to disappear completely. Moreover, there is responsibility attached – if move out you must, do it properly. Do not shortchange anyone or leave a mess behind. Do it with grace.

* * *

**And yes! Do not be too harsh on yourself.
It's fine if you gave your best.**

103

**In life, loyalties can shift
pretty quickly.**

* * *

Most people think that status of any form of relationship depends entirely on what two persons feel about it and bring 'to' it. What they don't factor in is the impact of a crucial intervening factor – circumstances. Yes, in a relationship, what goes on 'around' the two makes the decisive difference.

And who can control everything about everything around them? That's why all relationships, by nature, are vulnerable and variable. So what to do when storm of situations belittles strength of sentiments? Well, just hold your end of the rope as long and as tightly as you can, and hope (yet not expect) that…

* * *

…the other one reciprocates.

104

**If you respect your morning, the
whole day respects you.**

* * *

Unless you belong to the tribe of artists who get inspired at oddest hours or are one of the shift-workers who are resigned to their fate being governed by the planning department, you got to realize that the best way you can derive the best from your life is by giving your best to the early hours of the day.

With due respect to the temptation to squeeze every ounce from a day by staying up late, the fact is that the closest you are to almighty SUN's schedule, the better it is for you – in terms of both efficiency as well as effectiveness. Yup! There is something about being in synch with the rest of the ecology.

* * *

**Try it. If you don't find a difference,
you can always sleep over it.**

105

**Even Santa doesn't come
without a Claus(e).**

❋ ❋ ❋

In life, very few things are unconditional. For most of them, there are clear conditions. Those conditions are tacit and unsaid, left to be understood on your own. And not surprisingly, as long as you agree to conditions, you enjoy the privilege.

For instance, when the world gives money, it often takes your time away from you…When world gives fame, it often takes away your privacy…When world gives love, it often takes away your right to object…When world gives authority, it often takes away your freedom.

❋ ❋ ❋

**Well, let's plan to at times give…and not
take away much in return.**

106

**Never conclude that you know
a person well enough.**

* * *

Human mind is a puzzle that keeps changing. Moreover, functionally, it is a cylinder with a shifting base. On the top of it, a person also has three different identity-spheres – a public persona, a personal profile and a private self. Whoa! That renders every person a variable and never a constant.

So irrespective of the number of years you have known a person for or the amount of time you spend together, the fact is that 'you never really know a person well enough'. It surely is like an iceberg and you can only see the tip. But then what does it mean for us in intrapersonal & interpersonal terms?

* * *

**It means – "Always see people with
a certain curiosity". It helps.**

107

**After a point, most relationships tend to
turn merely functional in nature.**

* * *

The biggest challenge in a relationship is to retain the spark that you had at the start. Oh! And that's not easy. After all, everything natural is bound to change, and brain has an innate tendency to take things for granted so that it can save its processing power on that front and reallocate it as per need.

But in relationships, this stabilizing often leads to stagnancy. The partners become providers for each other or say they get into their respective roles. And then they have their set routines and rituals, and gradually that's all that amounts to life. Sadly, then the distance grows, and emotions recede.

* * *

**Invest in retaining freshness in a relationship
– Stable shouldn't mean…stale.**

108

**Sometimes the undeserving one
walks away with all the sympathy.**

* * *

In the realm of troubled relationships, it is almost impossible to determine who is actually the victim – the one who shouts in rage or the other who sobs all the time? The one who complains or the other who doesn't want to talk about it? The one who wants to end it or the other who wants it to continue?

It is such a complex web that what meets the eye seldom shows what is. There is a lot going behind and beneath – there are old scores settled, there are subtle games played, there are hidden agendas served, and there are scripted stories told. And amid all this, it is hard to know who did what…for what.

* * *

**That's why "Never pass a judgment unless
you have known enough".**

109

For many people out there, their relationship status actually is… "Somehow holding on".

* * *

It is strange how equations change in life. Now you can't live with "what" you once couldn't live without. It's cruelly ridiculous, but you go through it every day. And now you are too invested to leave…too settled to disrupt. There is far more at stake…far too much to simply walk away. So you continue…

You reckon you will somehow manage – at times by bearing…at times by ignoring; with an occasional tiff…or by reminding yourself "what if". And it works! But then…you begin to wonder if it's all worth it. You know what! There are no binary answers. It's a long and winding process of finding a solution.

* * *

Commit yourself to that process now, before it is too late for a discovery or a…recovery.

110

If you don't feel like working, remind yourself that there are "bills to be paid".

* * *

I am a great proponent of working with inspiration, however no one can depend entirely on inspiration for work, sometimes a healthy proportion of desperation is also good. The reason is simple. Inspiration and desperation are at best just triggers, what actually propels achievement is "perspiration".

So whether it is inspiration or desperation, their importance lies in getting the perspiration triggered. And once that happens, the pursuit gains its own momentum, and takes its own course. So if, in spite of inspiration, you feel lost, disillusioned, bored, sluggish or uninspired, just remember that…

* * *

…"bills to be paid" don't wait for you to feel a spark to go to work.

111

**Everyone deals with their pain in
their own unique way.**

* * *

Some people cry their heart out. Some people weep a silent tear. Some people lock themselves in their room. Some people scream at the top of their voice. Some people sip something that can help them forget or bear. Some people talk their way out of it. And then, some people…work their butt out.

Yes, work can be such a healer. It can hug you tight and let you in without asking any uncomfortable questions. It can soothe you. It can help you dispel the clouds of distress. It can help you deal with what you are not able to decipher or name. But I am afraid to say that… work cannot solve or resolve.

* * *

**Work can heal you, but then it's "you"
who has to heal what pains.**

112

Now, it'll be a rare privilege to have a partner who is "loving" yet has low maintenance…no melodrama…less fluctuation.

* * *

Most modern relationships seem to be coming straight out of either a sentimental serial of an Indian channel, or an American web-series' Indian imitation. No seriously! These days, there are two major formats in relationships – In one, partners are so obsessed with each other that they are suffocating each other by being together all the time or intertwining their lives needlessly.

And in the other type, partners are connected so superficially as if they have downloaded a trial version of some software and keep using it but keep clicking on 'Later' when there is a question about registering. My God, what madness! Polar opposites in same era. But you know what, then there are a few rare lucky relationships, in which, both partners know that love is…

* * *

…to anchor someone without cutting their wings.

113

"You will know when you will become"
is possibly every parent's patent line.

＊ ＊ ＊

And it isn't wrong for sure. When you become a parent, you know how tough it must have been for your dad or mom. When you become a leader, you know at times how lonely it can be at the top. When you are hit by lasting sadness, you know why depression is such a dreaded word.

That's why "empathy" is so important. Well, you may not be able to soothe everyone's pain or relieve them of it. And in fact, sometimes that pain could be unavoidable or necessary. Yet it is required to at least be respectful towards a person's unique circumstance and stance.

＊ ＊ ＊

Respect what someone goes through, even when
you don't know...what it is.

114

**When you express disagreement,
watch the other person carefully.**

❋ ❋ ❋

What do they say next? How do they behave? – Yup! People reveal their most genuine and intrinsic states and traits when their opinions are challenged; to the extent that, it is almost a litmus test for person's emotional environment as well as intellectual integrity.

Well, of course there is a rider here! When the challenge is explicitly offending or outright ridiculous, a knee-jerk reaction is understandable. However, though not conclusively, even then, the behavior does give a sneak peek into person's overall internal infrastructure.

❋ ❋ ❋

**So, next time, when this happens,
do observe them as well as ... yourself.**

115

Leaders are not supposed to be heroes, they are supposed to be "actors in a leading role".

* * *

Our society has an insatiable hunger for heroes. We are obsessed with "larger than life" characterization with backstories and anecdotes. That's why we are always looking for the new messiah… the next savior… the latest liberator. And then we bring the same tendency to… organizations.

So we treat individuals in leadership roles as the supreme souls incarnated in the sacred corner-offices. Apart from obvious ills like sycophancy and cartels, this also leads to the person at the top becoming conscious about impressions and imagery rather than roles and responsibilities.

* * *

Let's stop being hero-hungry, and transcend to 'respecting all roles', including… ours.

116

When you lose trust in your closest people,
it's the biggest loss incurred.

* * *

There are episodes in your life when you lose a lot, that too in every sense. While most of what is lost can be quantified or measured, some of it you cannot measure but is actually…major. It is the loss of trust in the near and dear ones you counted on.

You always felt they would stand by you, in your thick and thin. You always thought that they would shield you, support you or at the least soothe the hurt and the pain. But shockingly, they either witness like bystanders or ignore like strangers.

* * *

That's what makes you lose trust,
and with it… most of what matters.

117

**At some point, you have to begin to
look at your compromises as your choices.**

* * *

There are times when you have to comply with the call of the circumstance, and make a choice that otherwise you wouldn't have made. And you make that compromise as there is something at stake which, in the present circumstance, is more important than your like-dislike or comfort-discomfort.

However, the problem starts when the circumstance changes but you get locked in the choice. You can't bear anymore because now there is no good reason to do so, and you can't break free either because you have built an entire apparatus around the choice that you can't afford to dismantle.

* * *

**In such case, the only way out is to be 'all in'.
See it as your own, and settle.**

118

In life, some lines should be crossed only with this cognizance that once you cross them, there is no coming back.

* * *

Every choice shapes you. However, there are some choices that change you forever. Yes, the changes they elicit are irrevocable. Even if you come back to the same life circumstances afterwards, you don't remain the same "you". Something inside you touches the point of no return. So, is crossing those lines good or bad?

Well, that's not the point, because whether something is good or bad is always subject to which side you are on, and which angle you are looking from. But one thing is for sure – for better or worse, the transformation will be permanent.

* * *

And yes, do remember that from then onward, any new line that you draw shall be…vulnerable.

119

**If you don't know someone's story,
don't judge their character.**

* * *

People become what they become through an assembly line of coincidences and experiences. Yes, their choices do play an intervening role, yet there is still a lot that is beyond their scope of free-will – their parents, their backgrounds, their early influences, their acquaintances or their circumstances.

And though they always have a choice to make and an option to click, even their options are limited by the roll of the dice. Yup! "What they become" is rooted in where they come from and what came to them. That's why it is important to not make opinions about people without knowing their context.

* * *

**After all, in any script, characters
always emerge from the plot.**

120

Kids suffer most when they get "polar-opposite inputs regarding life" from each of their parents.

* * *

And here I am not talking about difference of opinions but difference of approaches towards basic matters like... managing oneself, relating to people, and living life. Yes, regarding this, if they receive absolutely contrasting inputs then they are not able to bear this ambiguity, and eventually suffer.

In fact, I am not talking only about kids. I am actually talking about any form of combined creation – whether it is a proposition, a project, or... an organization. When the co-creators have a clashingly different conception of the same thing in their minds then eventually the creation suffers.

* * *

Differences are healthy, but not in the very fundamental sense.

121

Sometimes irritating people pass off as stylish just because they have success on their side.

* * *

Success has an amazing way of changing people's perceptions. It acts almost like a seal of approval acknowledged universally. With its stamp on someone, suddenly the same person begins to seem very different. Yup! Even the profane begins to look profound…even the frivolous begins to look fabulous.

And then begins what I call "alignment of idiocy" – a cascading change of perceptions creeping into everyone's mind. You see the story of 'king with the new invisible clothes' getting enacted on demand. Well, though seemingly it looks harmless, it all leaves virtues of authenticity and merit gasping.

* * *

**There is no doubt that success deserves respect.
However, it doesn't deserve…reverence.**

122

**In life, never forget those who
stood by you when it mattered.**

* * *

Some people don't hug you tight or wish you bright. They don't meet you often or call you even. They don't give you gifts or accompany on your drifts. They don't send you jokes or respond to your pokes. They don't make promises or sing your praises. Yet…they are more special than the ones who do all this.

And what makes them special is that they stood by you when you needed it the most. They did it quietly but firmly. They never said big things; they did those small things which no one else did. They were the ones who held you without even touching you. They were the ones who backed you so you can be back.

* * *

**Never be ungrateful to them. You stand today,
because they stood by you.**

123

**At times you know you are better than the guy who won.
And that…it's not over yet.**

* * *

Sometimes you lose to someone, not on merit but on circumstance.
You run out of luck at the time when it matters the most, and from
then onward, the roll of the dice just doesn't go your way. And though
you keep trying to have a foot in the door, by then, the other guy has
grabbed his chance.

And then you see him celebrate. You see him take a bow and sign
off with the applause that you know you rightfully deserved. And a
part of you sobs quietly in the noise of firecrackers, unnoticed and
undone. But then, you lift your face up, look at the heavens…

* * *

**And tell the guy up there…
"I will be back".**

124

**Sometimes, something happens, and
you are never the same "you" again.**

* * *

Some experiences jolt you to the core. Not in the sense of making you
shout like hell but in the sense of making you numb like shell. You are
so taken aback by the suddenness and the force of it that you aren't
able to even register what has happened. It just leaves you stunned
like a stone.

But as the tides recede, you begin to realize the enormity of what
it has done to you. It changes something deep inside you. And that
change is not incremental or reversible; it is actually eruptive and
irrevocable. Yup, it changes something about you mentally, that too
fundamentally.

* * *

**And then you wonder why you were
"what you were" before it happened.**

125

**Don't accommodate people to an extent that
it comes back to haunt you.**

* * *

Being nice can be a big disadvantage. Because you are sensitive and considerate, you go out of the way to take care of people, adapt to create synchrony, ignore their idiocy, overlook their arrogance, and compensate for their incompetence. Yup! You deploy extra maturity to somehow make things work.

And that extra maturity doesn't come from nowhere. You sacrifice your natural flow, you curb your obvious reactions, you postpone your instinctive preferences, and you even go against your very nature. And it all takes a toll. However, even after all the toll, it is seldom respected, remembered or reciprocated.

* * *

**So, set limits for accommodating. Else…
people will gladly walk over you.**

126

**Three cardinal sins of SPIRITUALITY are –
EXPLAIN, PASS ON & INDUCT.**

❋ ❋ ❋

Yesterday, a dear one was discussing with me about how spirituality can be really hollow and shallow, and was urging me to explain how it is not. In that context, I told her the words in the first line – The three cardinal sins of SPIRITUALITY are – EXPLAIN, PASS ON, and… INDUCT. This is how it goes…

When I feel a feeling or experience an experience, it is not hollow or shallow to me, as I feel/experience it in my physiology. But when I try to EXPLAIN it through words, PASS it ON through methods or try to INDUCT others into it through systems, then it runs a risk of becoming hollow, shallow and manipulative.

❋ ❋ ❋

**Well, I've already committed first sin.
Now let me stop before other two.**

127

**World remembers worst of the actors
and forgets best of the critics.**

* * *

Well, I do not doubt the importance of critics. I mean a critic who is knowledgeable and gives inputs to improve your work or further your domain is a great value-addition. However, some people will always comment on your work without the sincerity and bona fide intention required behind it.

Interestingly, some of them will do so because they want to gain attention – from you, and from those who are paying attention to your work. These critics (rather commentators) are actually "wannabes" who want to do what you are doing or wish to get what you are getting. So when such people comment…

* * *

**Take it as a compliment that
"you are doing a good job".**

128

**In parenting, one's negligence should not be
overcompensated by other's indulgence.**

❋ ❋ ❋

It is not required to do a right for every wrong. This unnecessary
itch to match every balance sheet doesn't work well in life. At times,
it is prudent to choose the apt time and proper way to balance
'what wasn't done'. And this is equally true for leadership, teaching,
mentoring and most of all… parenting.

Well, unknowingly, at times parents vie for child's affection, and often
one takes another's miss as a chance to tilt the balance. Due to this
(and of course due to natural parental affection/concern), for one
parent's "not being there", the other one overcompensates, and sows
seeds for future problems.

❋ ❋ ❋

**So, avoid overcompensating. One's negligence is best filled by
other's attention. That's about it.**

129

**Sometimes people no longer miss you
the way you miss them.**

* * *

Even when two persons have the same emotion towards each other, they do not necessarily have the same intensity as well. You could be in pangs of love or throes of longing, and the other person may be feeling the same emotion but not equally. This is where you need to develop an important insight.

Feelings are seldom binary – on "On/off" mode. Instead, they have a regulator attached. And that regulation is subject to many aspects – circumstances, priorities, experiences, influx of new people, change in one's nature etc. So you shouldn't expect that the things between the two will never change.

* * *

**Everything changes. Get used to it;
and don't create fuss unnecessarily.**

130

**At times, love is such a mundane word
for what you feel for someone.**

* * *

You just struggle to define what exactly it is – you feel a strong connection, you are attached to them, you feel restless if they are sad, you want them to be happy, you like to hear their voice, you trust them implicitly, you tell them first when you have something to say, and you look for reasons to be with them.

Still, there is hardly a wish to make them yours, there is barely an urge to possess, there is seldom any jealousy for ones who share them with you, and there is rarely a romantic ripple escalating into a fleshly yearning. Well, there's just one desire – to have them alongside as you walk through life's journey.

* * *

**At times, love is such a mundane word
for what you feel for someone.**

131

**Some things aren't meant to be searched outside
but to be decided inside.**

❋ ❋ ❋

Most people are obsessed with the need for information even in the contexts where insights are needed more. Yes, you can't expect to find answers of everything outside, especially of the questions which are existential. And before you cringe, let me clarify that existential doesn't mean philosophical or abstract.

Existential means "concerned with the essence", so existential questions pertain to the root of a matter – the basis. Generally, they are not what or how but "why" questions. And it is logical that you can only find answers to these existential questions where actually your world exists – inside you.

❋ ❋ ❋

**Yup! At times, it is important to
close the eyes and… scan the disk.**

132

**Kindness is doing good to someone
you don't expect to meet again.**

* * *

The other day, rain was in the air, and traffic was picking up. As I drove towards a square, an old man was crossing the road. He looked at me, and with a dominance befitting his *age*, he showed his palm to me, signaling to wait. I could have accelerated to pass quickly, but I stopped, and so did two more cars. Well, as he crossed the road, an elevating smile was visible on his face.

His smile reminded me of an old *ad* of a bike, in which a young couple is riding on the bike, with girl holding the boy tightly from behind. Suddenly they see an unrelated old man coming. As the old man notices the couple, the girl gradually pulls back her arms, folds her hands behind her back and bows slightly as if wishing. Well, as the couple passes him, old man smiles a touched and touching smile.

* * *

**Individualism is good, yet how about mixing some
old-school *kindness and respect* to make some old people smile.**

133

**The only version of your life that's true
is the one that's happening to you.**

* * *

Fantasy is always beautiful – it is meant to be; else no one is idiot enough to put aside "what's happening" to transport themselves to a virtual vision of "what might happen". And this fantasy has immense utility. It has an anesthetic effect on the paining heart and a stimulating effect on a craving mind.

But how will that fantasy become a reality? Well, only by being rooted right here, in the slippery sands of the present moment, because only in the womb of this moment lies the fetus of tomorrow. This moment is the one that, through its umbilical, nourishes that unborn to help it take birth.

* * *

**So come back O traveler of tomorrow!
It's here that the journey begins.**

134

**The most important job of a leader is to
mold people without… breaking them**.

* * *

And for that, a leader has to blend what is *seemingly separated*. Yes, a leader has to be friendly yet firm… strong yet accommodating… participative yet decisive… mature yet enthusiastic…

…empathetic yet objective…'in role' yet genuine… progressive yet rooted… accessible yet enigmatic. But for that, the leader has to first be *integrative inside*.

* * *

**After all, you can't lead people unless
you lead yourself first**.

135

**Sometimes, you win outside,
and lose inside.**

* * *

Life can be really testing even for a normal person. And it is not about major events like big diseases, great debts or painful divorces. It is about dealing with those small stressors which, in the larger scheme of things, look embarrassingly insignificant; but one by one, cumulatively, become heavy.

It is about lack of sleep, acidity, adjusting with awkward silence at home, a nonchalant loudspeaker across the street, remembering dates of the due payments, finding a space for parking, ignoring an annoying coworker, or weathering a traffic jam while the spondylitis has flared up.

* * *

**You handle it all. But it all adds up, to cause
an internal imbalance. Take care.**

136

Not everyone will respect your struggle. So don't start *"look what I have been through..."* at every opportunity.

* * *

Everyone has a story and every person is the protagonist of his or her own story. And because people tell their stories from their angle so all the characters are aligned in the narrative to serve that angle. That's why everyone thinks that he has been through a lot, or she has seen the worst, or he has fought alone, or it was only her guts to survive in spite of all that happened.

Moreover, all of us secretly compare our struggles with each other's. That's why it is difficult to bear someone telling (and subtly glorifying) his collection of the stories from a hero's diary. That's why we interject, dissuade, divert, or every now and then subtly place a story or two from our own proud collection. So... don't start that epic on the slightest of excuses.

* * *

And if a rare person will really respect your struggle then you won't have to start the story. Actually they will not leave unless you tell it completely.

137

Some people are eternal misfits.
They are forever in search of a place for themselves.

* * *

Right from the beginning, they are different – a tad too sensitive, an ounce too observant, a bit too radical. They are not geniuses, though the proposition that they could become remains untested. But anyways, they are too shy to declare that or cajole others into believing it.

Initially, they pretend they can comply with the norm of the normal, but the fact is that a part of them is never in it. In reality, they are always looking for a niche which they can call their own – a part on the planet where they can come into their own and unleash their originality.

* * *

Well, if you know one, help them.

138

**In relationships, long silences are often
muted screams.**

❋ ❋ ❋

There are times when a person conveys pain or discomfort repeatedly, and in every which way possible. Yet the other person either doesn't listen, or listens but ignores or doesn't understand the severity. This happens due to other person's insensitivity, rigidity, negligence or different priorities.

Whatever is the reason, it devastates the one who is more sensitive, adjusting, involved and committed. It is like left stranded in a jungle with sun going down; or being too invested to withdraw. This deadlock and imminent dead-end can take a real toll. And often, you have nothing left to say to the other person.

❋ ❋ ❋

Hence the silence.

139

**The other day, someone asked me...
"So what are you chasing in life?"**

* * *

What am I chasing? Riches? Or respect? Or status? Or satisfaction? Or significance? What am I chasing? Why do I get up every morning and work? What am I chasing? You know what! I have no delusion of being unique, or better than others, or a special one in the making.

Yes, like *everyone else*, I want to be spotted...I want to be endorsed. But honestly, that's not the biggest kick I get out of what I do. Actually, every morning I get up and work because I want to express myself, unleash what's inside, do what I truly believe in, and hope that...

* * *

**I will be spotted for 'that'...
endorsed for 'that'.**

140

When someone is going through a difficult phase, be very careful about what you say to them; as they are going to remember it forever.

❋ ❋ ❋

It is tough to deal with someone who is going through a tough time. Yes, when someone goes down, his sensitivity-level tends to go up. He (or she) becomes so touchy that at times you wonder if he is in fact searching for an excuse to get hurt. And in such a situation, one wrong or unkind word can leave its impression like a foot-print on a wet cement patch.

Well! With time, either the tide will throw him up as it turns, or he will swim his way out of it. But now, something peculiar will happen – he will understand that you did not mean to hurt when you had said 'that'…he will agree with your reasons to say it…he will acknowledge all the right things you said and did before and after 'that' thing… and eventually he will even forgive you for what you had said. However…

❋ ❋ ❋

… he will 'never forget' what you had said.

141

**There is no mortal who
has never erred.**

❊ ❊ ❊

Erring is an integral part of growing and maturing. But what people don't understand is that it's not the erring per se, but the introspection subsequent to erring that helps you grow and mature. Without cycle of analysis -> realization -> amendment -> application, a person only goes one step further and two steps back. And that's when we err in the literal sense of the word.

However, to analyze, a person needs to first learn to dissociate 'what he has done' from 'who he is'. This separation of performance from the performer is a prerequisite. Without it, a person only becomes defensive or dejected after the very step of analysis; and the next three steps go out of the window. That's where your self-esteem comes into play. And as I often say…

❊ ❊ ❊

**Self-esteem is how you feel 10 minutes after
failing, falling, erring, losing, or being denied or mocked.**

142

Someone told me that "someone less deserving has reached where I deserve to be". I thanked the person for the compliment and then… disagreed completely.

* * *

I firmly believe that, when someone reaches somewhere legitimately, it is always… well-deserved. I mean, there must surely be something that he or she has that others don't. I call it talent-blinded-ness. Yes, even if you've got more talent, the other person must have had some other thing to compensate for it.

It could be tenacity. It could be temperament. It could be timing. It could be tact. Or it could be a trump at the top. Whatever it is, something must have gone behind attaining and retaining it; and that something must have taken toll on that person. After all, nothing comes or stays for free.

* * *

So, let's not stereotype struggle; and let's respect people for what they have.

143

You can't expect to know your true self through the selfies you take.

* * *

"Knowing yourself" is not reserved for domains of philosophy or spirituality. It has amazing utility in life. And contrary to the popular belief, it does not require sitting in the Buddha pose and tapping into the chakras. With due respect to that method, the fact is that there is more to it.

In life, knowing yourself requires conscious tracking of your journey…through continuous analysis of your experiences…in the light of causes, consequences and changes. Yes, it is about deliberating on "what happened" in terms of "why it happened", "what it led to" and "how it shaped you".

* * *

And that requires, not looking at the camera, but looking at the…looker.

144

In relationships, when you exercise your right to move away then you have to *respect* other's right to move on.

❋ ❋ ❋

In a relationship, when you choose to leave someone somewhere, you cannot expect the person to stay there, waiting for you to come back – that too when there is no premise that you will…or no promise about when. After all, that person also has only one life to live…only one chance to take this journey… only one shot at happiness.

Yes, it is important to remember that you don't own anyone forever. People are their own properties. When they lend you a part of their selves then it is their choice to do so. They can't be emotionally blackmailed to forego their right on their selves and their lives. It is the only right they have in a world where there nothing else is certain. Respect that.

❋ ❋ ❋

**So, when you leave someone but want to begin again,
then you have to… begin again.**

145

**Sometimes, your life's balance hinges on
your ability to bear and ignore.**

* * *

There are times when you end up getting blocked in an arrangement
where you can't change the people around you because maintaining
status quo is the need of the hour, and also you can't get back at them
because you are too sensitive to stand awkwardness of working or
living in a strained environment.

Now begins the test of your maturity. You want to complain but you
don't. You want to shout but you can't. You want to leave but that just
isn't an option. So then you breathe in breathe out heavily to tolerate
the heaviness in your head. But then there are days when it gets too
weighty for your head.

* * *

**On such days, remind yourself of
"why" you are doing it, and then... do it.**

146

If you want to own every room you are in, it spells 't.r.o.u.b.l.e.' for your relationships.

* * *

Some people always want to be at the center of every circle. They sulk when the spotlight shifts. They become out of place if they are not getting attention. They can't lose their identity and become "just one of them" in a room full of happy people. They have a need to be seen and heard all the time.

Such people find it hard to build a happy family, a fulfilled relationship, or a feel-good team. However, if they are lucky, they get people who bear them and make adjustments to somehow manage to create a sense of normalcy in their apparatus. But such victims of self-importance must understand that…

* * *

To have colors in your life, you have to be, not a commanding brush, but an accepting canvas.

147

**Don't make people uncomfortable if
they don't follow your advice.**

✳ ✳ ✳

Unless you are in official capacity or have a stake in the matter, you have to let people use their right to "not listen" to you even if you are right. This is true even when people had come on their own to ask for your advice. After all, it's their life and thus their prerogative to choose their pick.

So don't fill them with guilt of not paying heed just because you want to take an indirect pride in being proven right. Please understand that every advice, no matter how good it is, has to be seen in the light of feasibility, familiarity and fitness in one's larger scheme of things.

✳ ✳ ✳

**Inspire faith and trust in people,
not guilt and regret.**

148

It's amazing how one person's trauma is merely an incident for another person, and just a piece of news for yet another.

❋ ❋ ❋

The pain of what happens to a person is sadly now beginning to get limited to that one person. And why so? Well, because we are so inundated with one information after another…one idea after another…one impulse after another, that it's now rare that something enters our mental systems and commands our exclusive attention for long enough to invoke true empathy.

Yes, in our over-stimulated society, we are missing out on depth of experiences, and are growing even shallower in experiencing vicarious feelings – feelings felt by witnessing another person go through an experience. And the most important way to restore that genuinely human quality of compassion is to keep a tab on our craving for diversity of information and instead strive for depth of it.

❋ ❋ ❋

The fact is that…"Information can never be a substitute for immersion".

149

**To get what you want, you have to
first know what it is.**

* * *

The reason why most people get disillusioned in the pursuit of success is because they have not really defined it. It remains a sketchy notion in their minds that keeps changing all the time. I do respect that definition is supposed to change at various stages of life or after a life-changing event; and it is also equally important to keep raising the benchmarks.

However, the definition cannot be short-term or short-lived. And it also cannot be based on a 'socially constructed' idea of what it is. It has to emerge from within you, and should be a manifestation of your values, talents and intrinsic desires. Call it vision, mission or some other good-sounding word, the only criterion is that it should truly represent you.

* * *

**After all…what you want
should come from who you are.**

150

**You can't divide life into
weekdays and weekends.**

❊ ❊ ❊

"Monday Blues" is a reality. And it has less to do with one's
vocation and more about the incapacitating mindset inherited from
generations of civilized humans. It's true that not everyone enjoys
what they are doing to earn a living or preparing to be able to do so;
and many are compelled to pick what's available.

However, let's pick what's still within our choice – our attitude. Let's
not just look for meaning but "create meaning" by adjusting our
aspirations in tune with our abilities and conditions. Let's bring
an attitude that helps us see our life as one coherent story flowing
through our days with ebb and flow.

❊ ❊ ❊

**Rather than waiting for life to come to us,
let's fill it in all ordinary moments.**

151

**The only way to learn a new thing is to
keep doing it until it becomes old.**

* * *

So, why do most people fail to develop new habits? Well, beginning to develop a habit is thrilling. After all, you are doing something new; so you feel excitement, hope and optimism. You feel a sense of control on your destiny. You feel important. You feel liberated. You feel creative. You feel powerful. You feel... good.

But then after sometime, the newness goes away. Now, there is hardly any excitement. It's monotony. It's drudgery. It's ritual. It's repetitive. It's routinized. And though it is still challenging, the problem is that challenge is not fresh – it's stale. You feel...not so good. Yes, people fail to develop new habits, *not* because it is *tough* to do so, but because it is boring to do so.

* * *

**Embrace boredom,
embrace change.**

152

Biggest curse for modern human is not the desire to multitask but the ability to multitask.

* * *

As I often discuss in my workshops on social and emotional intelligence, multitasking is about sacrificing depth for width. Yes, you shouldn't do something just because you can do it. In fact, often a greater willpower is required not in doing something you can't do but in not doing something that you can do. As I often tell people… "professionalism is essentially the ability to postpone pleasure".

Anyways, so this is how the battle inside capable persons typically goes: "There are so many things that they want to do. And all of them look important. When they begin to do one thing, the thought of 'doing the next thing' or 'not doing the other thing' keeps intervening. They feel as if something is slipping out of their hands – time or opportunity. And that makes them even more restless".

* * *

Well, problem is not that you want everything. Problem is that you want everything together and now.

153

**Sometimes all you want is to get back at
people who were mean towards you.**

* * *

Even when you know that they were mean for all sorts of reasons:
Some of them did it unintentionally…some of them were venting
their venom out…some of them were victim of their own
circumstances…some of them did it out of jealousy…some of them
did it out of frustration…some of them badly wanted to feel good
about themselves…

Then some of them wanted to get even with you… some of them
wanted to test you…some of them simply wanted to hurt you… and
some of them were just wired to be so. Yup! Sometimes all you want
is to get back at people who were mean towards you. But then you
realize that their reasons to be mean were far more valid than yours.

* * *

**So…you drop
the idea.**

154

It is important to travel, as it helps you dismantle the notion that "your world is just some relationships… a pursuit called work… and a concept called home".

* * *

When you travel, you recognize the vastness of the world we live in…the variety of situations life can conceive…the vividness of experiences on offer…and the value of human-connect beyond one's concentric orbits.

It challenges you and introduces you to yourself in a way nothing else can. It makes you unlearn and relearn. And it helps you review your perspective and restore your sanity. But most importantly, it also helps you miss what you are away from.

* * *

Yes, it is important to travel, as it helps you realize the truth that "your world is just some relationships… a pursuit called work… and a concept called home".

155

**When you are picking a fight everywhere,
it is indicating that the fight is… inside you.**

* * *

There are times when you feel that everyone is against you. Everyone is selfish. Everyone is using you. Everyone lets you down. No one understands you. No one values you. No one has paid back for your goodness. They all are same. But what you don't realize is that 'you' are the only common factor in all your relationships.

So some introspection is due – Do you have an idealistic definition of what relationships should be like? Are you expecting those things from people which they can't give? Are you unnecessarily giving too much and that's why what you get always seems too less? Well, in either case, it is not about them, it's about you.

* * *

**If everyone is making you unhappy then
they don't need to make you. Probably…you already are.**

156

**You can't hope to solve a personal problem
while trying to manage your impression.**

❊ ❊ ❊

Due to the nature of my work, people often ask for inputs on their intrapersonal & interpersonal problems. Ironically, when I hear them expressing their problems, often I find that they do not tell their problems honestly. Actually they try to manage their impressions while presenting their problem.

They use stylish words to seem well-read; or use subjectivity to avoid embarrassment; or frame issue in a manner that shows them in good light; or check their expressions to not let sophistication go down; or censor their versions to not look weak or dumb; or present in a "leading way" to evoke sympathy.

❊ ❊ ❊

**Sadly, when they do that, it becomes
another part of the problem.**

157

"He is past his prime…"
I heard them saying about him.

❋ ❋ ❋

And they were not talking about some cricketer. They were talking about a man whose journey I have followed closely over the years, right through his pretty high 'ups' and equally low 'downs'. He came…he saw…he conquered. And then one day, he threw caution to the wind, to only be hit by a strong storm…falling steeply from dizzy heights…to find himself in a state they called "way past his prime". You know what! One day they will say this about me… about you.

And the worst part is that probably they will be right. On that day, don't sulk or fume. Close your eyes, and then later go for a walk, and introspect. If you think what they say has merit then 'take a break' or 'revive' or 'reinvent' or 'reposition' or 'find where you can be of value even with your averageness'. And if nothing works then walk away into the woods with grace…

❋ ❋ ❋

…to find new
meanings and purposes.

158

**Sometimes, some people's behavior
towards you is simply toxic.**

❋ ❋ ❋

And they behave in that manner not because you did something
to deserve such treatment or because they are going through a
bad phase or because they are transferring to you the trauma that
someone else has caused them or because they themselves are
suffering. They behave that way because… that's the way they are.

Call it inherited genes, early upbringing or for that matter plain
'negative experiences', yet let's face it – they are like this. Now you
can have three ways to deal with it – 'get away from them as early as
possible' or 'maintain a firm 'stay around but don't cross boundary'
stand or 'increase will power to such an extent that it ceases to
bother you'.

❋ ❋ ❋

**Well, such people do change eventually. All you've to see is whether
you have enough reasons to wait and bear till then.**

159

**Data can't give you empathy. You got to
listen to your customers' stories.**

❋ ❋ ❋

I am a strong believer in utility of data and all that can be done with it. I also know "what can't be measured can't be managed". Thus, an attempt to quantify is an important endeavor. But it shouldn't become a crusade…an obsession. And it should also not be seen as a panacea for all 'business and management' problems.

Well, business doesn't take place in our cabins, it takes place in the customer's mind. That's why, to see how our work is perceived and the impact it makes, we have to listen to customer's stories. And I am not talking about seeing it as a case to be later used as a testimonial. I am talking about listening to really… "listen".

❋ ❋ ❋

**Stories are also data. It's just that while listening,
you have to forget that they are.**

160

**At times all you want is to
go away from all the melodrama around.**

* * *

There is a difference between sensitivity and melodrama. Sensitivity is about "paying attention to and taking care of" even the smallest of things - Apparatus, methods, mannerisms, hints, words, tone, gestures, and even their interconnections. All matter. In short, a place for everything and everything at its place. In spite of this, in sensitivity, you let small things remain small, and do not blow them out of proportions.

On the contrary, in melodrama, you do not let small things remain small; you blow them out of proportions to make them big. Every 'out of place' thing is overhyped, every word is analyzed threadbare, every gesture is taken as a hint, every aberration is seen as a mistake, and what you miss suddenly becomes the most sacrosanct. And alas, often it is confused as sensitivity.

* * *

**Well, what separates ugly melodrama from beautiful sensitivity
is just one thing…'Over'.**

161

**There are times when all you keep asking yourself is…
"Where did I go wrong?"**

* * *

You did not leave any stone unturned…you did not leave any aspect unattended. You preempted…you tried to offset…you tried to prevent. You adjusted…you changed…you sacrificed. You talked…. you listened…you kept quiet. You were always there – right there. And yet…

…you are standing there stranded – with a pale face, heaving chest, shivering hands, dry lips, and moist eyes. You know that's not what you had signed up for…that's not why you were bearing all that with a smile…that's not what you imagined it would come down to.

* * *

**But all that remains is 'questions' – questions
whose answers don't matter anymore.**

162

**In life, every relationship introduces
you to yourself in a unique way.**

❋ ❋ ❋

If it weren't for it, you would never come to know that you can be
so strong yet so weak, so giving yet so insecure, so adjusting yet so
possessive, so patient yet so impulsive, so dignified yet so frivolous,
so clear yet so muddled, so decisive yet so tentative, so together yet so
lonely, so happy yet so sad, so complete yet so inadequate.

Yes, it is as if you are on a journey within. So, when you love, you
feel…you gush…you care…you share…you smile…you sob…you
laugh…you cry…you regret…you rejoice.

❋ ❋ ❋

**But don't forget to also…
learn from it.**

163

In life, there will always be negative events. But do not let them become negative experiences.

* * *

I am a firm believer in the saying "experience is not what you come across. It is what you do with what you come across". Yes, you may never have control over what happens to you, but more often than not, you can still have control over what you let it do to you. Thus, whenever you go through something unpleasant, try to see it in a light that makes it look less dark.

See it as a learning you required at this point of time, a teaching that was long due, a cue for solving a problem, a hint for making a decision, a nudge from destiny towards a preordained route, or simply a message from the guy up-there that will make sense sometime down the line. So, a 'negative feeling' could be a natural first reaction, but a 'positive inference' should be the end-point. This way, you won't grow cynical with every passing year.

* * *

Rather, you will become a person who has been there…done that.

164

**Democracy is good only when people put
larger-good above what's good for them.**

* * *

Over the years I have realized that you can't make people do even the right thing, because they have different definitions of what's right and those definitions are governed less by what's the best way to serve and more by what serves them best.

That's perfectly understandable because of course everyone has a right to exercise one's discretion and maximize one's chances of addressing one's priorities. However, problem starts when people are in a setup which puts them in a network of interdependence. Because then…all of them can at best attain good and can never reach the best.

* * *

**And then, full-form of TEAM becomes
'Together Everyone Attains Mediocrity'.**

165

**Some relationships are best
left unanalyzed.**

❊ ❊ ❊

I have known both of them for years. Just when I think they are inseparable, they diverge. Just when I think they are incompatible, they unite. Just when I think they don't care for each other, one of them holds the fort for the other. Just when I think they have matured, they fall out.

They keep leaving and coming back, saying goodbyes and then being a call away. They aren't bonded by a bond with a name and they are least interested in naming the bond that binds them together. Well, when I last saw them, I asked her "Who are you of each other?" She smiled and said…

❊ ❊ ❊

"…the missing piece of the puzzle".

166

In life, how you feel depends on what you focus on.

* * *

In your world, there will always be people who won't like you much. They will make you feel small. They will not acknowledge or respond. They will ignore or neglect. They will criticize and even vilify. They will give wry smiles or no smiles at all. They will compare you and even demean. They will undermine your potential and exaggerate your flaws. They will play games. They will target you and will not miss any chance to single you out.

And then there will always be people who will like you. They will make you feel good about yourself. They will expect good from you and will wish good for you. They will forget your failures and forgive your mistakes. They will smile at you and will talk nice about you behind your back. They will refer opportunities to you and will spread the good word. They will remind you of your glory and will encourage you for excellence.

* * *

The best way to get fulfillment, happiness and success in life is to stay cordial towards first type of people and focus on second type of people.

167

Where is my…'me'?

* * *

Have you seen it? Because I haven't for a while. Probably I forgot it at home when I had to be the 'mature' one to compensate for the stubborn ones around, or possibly lost it at the office when I had to align with others for maintaining stability, or maybe left it on the sofa when I was bearing the over-smart ones in the name of etiquette…

…or perhaps put it under the pillow when I got up tired and quietly began the day's chores after a sleepless night wrestling with my own mind. Yes, I guess it must be at one of those places, or may be a part of it at each one of them. Well, if you find it somewhere then…

* * *

**…still please don't bring it back…as
I am trying to learn to live without it.**

168

**Sometimes it takes all you've got…
to keep the wolves away.**

* * *

In the world around us, there are many people who are sitting on a tragedy from past, a trauma of some sorts – a misfortune…a betrayal…or a mistake. Beneath the façade of 'all is well now', the truth is that they still struggle to maintain normalness inside. There are nights when the ghosts from the past scare their sleep away, and there are mornings when they have to literally pull themselves out of bed to enter the world outside their rooms.

They are always on the verge of slipping back into the valleys which they have climbed breathlessly to come to the ground. Every setback sets them back, and every comment of criticism sends them back into the whirls of self-pity. Their experiences have made them oversensitive, and the distrust they feel because of being let-down so often by both man & god has made them vulnerable to trusting wrong people again. It is a daily struggle that will only end with life. Ironically, those who are lucky to have a normal life till now can never understand how it feels.

* * *

**And unfortunately…nor can
the sufferers ever tell.**

169

**A peculiar feeling which
most of us have is that…**

* * *

…we are happy, but not happy enough… we are successful, but not successful enough… we are known, but not known enough… we have come a long way, but not far enough… we earn decent, but not decent enough…

…we look good, but not good enough… we feel fine, but not fine enough… we are doing well, but not well enough. Well, that's not the problem. The *problem* is that we don't understand that…

* * *

…nothing is ever 'enough'.

170

**It is not the lack of talent or technique that blocks growth,
it is the lack of…temperament.**

❊ ❊ ❊

Every domain has a peculiar set of qualities required to sustain
excellence in it. However, there is an important part of that repertoire
which people tend to ignore – the temperament. I have always
believed that this one thing is what makes all the difference, but sadly
I see people not seeing it.

I have met researchers who are not curious…teachers who are not
learners…managers who are not empathetic…doctors who are not
listeners…and writers who are not readers. And when they ask me
why they are not growing any more, then I get amazed on how they
cannot see the obvious reason. Yes, people rise due to talent and excel
due to technique, but they progress due to their temperament.

❊ ❊ ❊

**When you work on it,
it works for you.**

171

**They rightly say… "First you make choices,
and then choices make you".**

* * *

Moreover, sometimes you can't see the chain of consequences
a choice has. For instance, you don't realize but one of the most
important choices you will ever make is when you will say…"I do".
Yes, the day you choose your life-partner, in a way, you also choose…

…your future family-structure…your future career-pattern…the sort
of (and size of) friend circle you will have…the kind of (and number
of) kids you will have…the kind of schedule you will follow…the
kind of neighborhood you will live in…the kind of places you will
visit…the kind of things you will spend your money on…the kind of
health-issues you will face…and even the life-span you will have, and
the amount of life you will have in it.

* * *

**So, before you say "I do", do remember that you are making not
just a choice for your life, but also the choice of your life.**

172

Helping someone get over sadness is an effort…but helping someone overcome depression is a process.

* * *

Sadness is different from depression. When you lose something or someone or simply lose, then it is natural to be sad and it does run its due course. However, depression is slightly different. A person begins to get depressed due to one of the three reasons…when he feels lonely, when he feels there is nothing good about him, or when he feels he is stuck and has no future.

And thus there are obvious ways to address these three reasons – by kindling his belief in your unconditional support…by pointing-out and highlighting his good aspects…and by giving hope and helping him chart out a path for future. And there are times when you have to do all three simultaneously, because depression is additive – it runs in a loop.

* * *

That's why it is important to not let a person go in depression rather than to try and get one out of it.

173

The most peculiar thing about relationships is that "two persons with *different* pasts come together to build a *common* future".

* * *

And for most people, that past doesn't pass away. It has shaped their personalities…it has influenced their perceptions…it must be governing their behavior…and it will interfere in their choices. Yes, that past seldom dies a timely death, and even if people try to kill it with reasoning, it reincarnates in various forms whenever the persons are vulnerable.

Well, the only way to counter past is that both persons envision a mutual future with such faith and in such details that the whole synergy of co-creation overpowers the residual effects of past by a significant margin. This requires both persons to make an equally strong commitment towards letting go of past and envisaging a future, rooted in present. Both persons need to think, talk, plan, discuss disagreements, persuade logically, create middle-paths and keep doing all this regularly…

* * *

…until years that have gone by are outnumbered by years being looked forward to.

174

**There are times when you don't want
to say anything to anyone…**

❋ ❋ ❋

You don't want to complain…or to demand… or to disagree… or to
question… or to object… or to discuss… or to explain…
or to express.

You don't even want anyone to understand…or to empathize…or to
help…or to reach out…or to care…or to realize…or to apologize…or
to believe…or to even know.

❋ ❋ ❋

**You just want to be quiet and alone…until…
it dies down inside on its own.**

175

**In love, it is natural to be interested in the person's past.
But you can't keep digging for details.**

* * *

Before you came in someone's life, the person must have had his or her share of emotional connections. So, it is highly unlikely that you are the first or the only one. While you should be 'sensitively and sensibly' available if the person wants to talk about it, you can't stay unduly curious about it. After all, even in the closest relationships, there is a line to be drawn – called respect. It is important to not wish to possess a person in entirety.

When someone says 'I am all yours', it can't mean what it sounds. Mind is like an iceberg and we all interact with each other's tips of those icebergs. It is every person's prerogative to decide how much of that iceberg he or she wants to share with you. Healthy relationships do have high self-disclosure; but it is well within a person's right to decide the pace and extent of that self-disclosure. Don't try to push the pace. And in any case, do remember…

* * *

**…"in relationship, beyond a point, you got to drop person's CV
and trust the performance appraisal."**

176

He looked visibly perturbed. So I put my hand on his shoulder and asked *"You must be clueless – isn't it?"* He nodded. I said *"tell me how you are feeling?"*

* * *

He said "I don't know. I really don't." I said "Ok! Does it feel this way?…"There are multiple fronts – with each of them pulling you towards it. You take care of one and the other front goes out of hand. When you begin to focus on one thing, the other things on the backburners keep disturbing. You decide priorities and then again end up surrendering to chaos – utterly exhausted.

There is always restlessness inside – to reach somewhere…to be somebody. There are always so many roles to play – each demanding your best. Everything is multilayered, and confusing. Nothing is black or white, everything is grey. There are no clear heroes, no clear villains. All mixed up. So much…and still you are expected to retain sanity, because if you lose it, you lose all".

* * *

Well, he looked at me in sheer astonishment, and said *"How do you know all this?"* I smiled, and said…*"Welcome to a man's world"*.

177

**I am a firm believer that
you should work even on your *average* days.**

❋ ❋ ❋

And you should do so in spite of the risk that you may end up producing just 'ordinary work' – far from the best that 'you are capable of' or 'are known for'. And there are two reasons for that. First, it introduces you to your average-ness which can be a really humbling and educating experience. It helps you take away that swagger from your walk and attribute your success to factors beyond your own self. It helps you appreciate significance of the process that makes you look good, and how with one missing step, your whole façade of invincibility can crumble. Yes, on such a day, you may lose face, but you will gain perspective.

Second, it helps you recruit in your repertoire the most important virtue of a professional – work ethic. Yes, for lasting success, there is nothing more significant than to 'show up more often'. In other words, it helps you bring age-old discipline and good-old 'sincerity' to your pursuits. It helps you assert to your own self that how you feel can govern how well you will work, but it cannot decide whether you will work or not.

❋ ❋ ❋

So, go out there, and stumble your way to success. You will neither look good nor feel good, but...it will 'be good' for you.

178

Life is most agonizing for those who have to fight
their demons while putting up an angelic face.

* * *

For years, I have had a rare privilege of being privy to the complex selves and cluttered minds behind the impressive personas and beautiful faces. As they open up, I can intensely feel their pain of not only living with that darker side but also of covering it up with the brighter one.

That's why I always say that most unfortunate are the ones who look normal but feel abnormal. They bear a curse of being too civilized for their own good. Behind their 'well-learnt words, well-timed wit and well-placed moves' lie the tiny pores from which their insecurities peek. They are Spider-men…

* * *

…caught in a web they have worked hard
to successfully build for themselves.

179

You fall in love with the way someone looks, smiles or talks; but you can only stay in love for the way a person thinks, behaves and listens.

* * *

In relationships, once the physics runs its course, the chemistry takes over. Yes, during a day, as you look at each other on numerous occasions, you don't look to appreciate the beauty of each other's face. You look to receive feedback, approval, empathy or just that pleasurable feeling of connectedness.

In such moments, it is not how that face is but what that face shows that decides how you feel. Well! Those moments define the texture of your relationship – which further translates into your fulfillment level and eventually the quality of your life. That's when a beautiful blank face becomes difficult to bear, or an average feel-good face becomes simply irresistible.

* * *

Yes, in relationships, you can't keep looking at each other. After sometime, you begin to look for something.

180

Patience boy…patience.

❋ ❋ ❋

I can see your jaw getting stiff…your breathing getting heavier…your chest heaving…your fists tightening up…your arms flexing…your nostrils flaring…your head beginning to ache. But then I can also see what all is there to lose…what all is there to save…what is at stake. So stay quiet. Just take a deep breath and swallow the ripples of irritation that you can feel rising towards throat.

Start thinking about something else – anything – just don't react. I know it is tough. But you always had a chance to walk out of this, yet you chose to stay for reasons which will sound silly to someone else but are important to you. I can feel that the force is strong enough to make you burst at the seams, but hold on. You have already put in the hard yards…now don't ruin all the hard work that has gone into it.

❋ ❋ ❋

Patience boy…patience; not just because you can't afford to fail, but also because…this too shall pass.

181

Forget about understanding or misunderstanding, at times you question your 'standing' in a relationship.

* * *

You begin to wonder – where do you stand…how important are you? You feel as if you are actually being taken for granted. You can sense that the other person's focus is elsewhere, and you feature lower in the list of priorities. But you wait because you have been promised that everything will soon be the way it used to be between you two.

To be honest, a part of you wants to confront… to demand what you think you deserve in the relationship. You want to ask the awkward questions, you want to say the hard things. But you don't. Because deep down inside you have faith that it is just a phase. It will pass. Well, there are times when your faith is proven to be right. But you never know. You could well be left stranded – punished for patience.

* * *

Still, in any case, you have to remember that it was your choice; and you can't blame the other person.

182

In life, there are times when you adjust because there is something you want to save – a relationship…an association…or an arrangement.

* * *

So, you adjust, and then adjust more – to avoid confrontation… to 'not hurt someone'… to let it pass… to 'not create a scene'… to maintain dignity… to give another chance… to respect what is at stake… or probably to avoid exploding and letting out your own worse side.

This goes on. And then one day, you look at yourself and go absolutely numb… you can't recognize the person in the mirror… you can't even recall who you originally were… what was it like to be your own self… who were you really at the core. That day, a realization dawns upon you that you have adjusted successfully to save 'that something'…

* * *

…but have ended up *losing* something more important – You.

183

**At times, getting away is
better than getting out.**

❋ ❋ ❋

In relationship problems, dialogue is important for diagnosis.
But when dialogue becomes a debate and starts moving towards
a dispute, then I firmly recommend that distance can be equally
effective for diagnosis. In other words, when casual confrontations
start taking magnitudes of continuous conflicts then rather than a
break-up, it is good to simply take a break.

It gives an opportunity to take stock of the situation with objectivity,
and to see the relationship in a new light – with lightness of a
beginner. It also helps one introspect, away from the heat of someone
breathing down one's neck all the time. Most importantly, this way,
one is also able to see life beyond that one relationship, and connect
that piece with other pieces in the puzzle. More often than not,
after that break, people return more balanced. However, if the rut
continues endlessly, then just remember...

❋ ❋ ❋

**On any day, breaking up is
better than...breaking down.**

184

**In future, the biggest problem in relationships
would be… overexposure.**

* * *

What people don't realize is that "love begins in your presence, but it grows in your absence". And these days, people are constantly in touch, through every possible medium. They are not giving each other any opportunity to miss each other.

The truth is that in love, you also fall in love with your image of your beloved. But it can only happen when there is a scope for imagination. Now, the relationships are far too stimulated. And when you carry each other everywhere, you run a risk of becoming a burden than a pleasure. So, save the charm in a relationship…

* * *

**…as it's damaging to overdo things that
one is supposed to do over a period of time.**

185

**The way you relate to people depends a lot
on who you relate them with.**

* * *

When you see someone, you subconsciously also see someone else
in him or her. And that shapes your connection. For instance, you
might dislike someone because you find glimpses of your dominating
parent, your bully sibling, your gossiping aunt, a teacher who didn't
select you for drama, a friend who ditched you, a boss who stole
your credit, a cousin you were always compared with; or even the
imaginary baba quoted by elders in your childhood.
The list is endless…

Similarly, you might like someone because you find glimpses of your
caring parent, supportive sibling, an encouraging uncle, a teacher
who complimented, a stranger who helped you selflessly, an ex you
miss, a loved one you lost or 'wanted but never had'; and even your
favorite actor, or lovable character from novel or serial. Again,
list has no end…

* * *

**Yes, the mind rewinds and reminds.
Stay cognizant of this fact in relationships.**

186

"The experiences that you choose make you a more successful person…and the experiences that you don't choose make you a more interesting person".

* * *

Most of the successful people are pretty boring. The reason is that in the pursuit of their success they become quite self-conscious – more guarded about themselves. On the other hand, the essential quality for being 'interesting' is the ability to take oneself lightly and to remain a little 'wide-eyed' about one's success. But the problem is that these successful people have been so obsessed with traits like 'focus', 'determination' and 'discipline' that they have been regulating the scope of their experiences – keeping it strictly around their choices.

And then there are people who know that their success has been an outcome of many variables 'beyond their influence' that came together just at the right time. They also worked hard, and continue to do so. But they remain a bit playful about their life. So they keep looking for and forward-to new experiences, with uncertain outcomes. In the process, such people 'learn humility to stay unaffected' and 'earn anecdotes to outlast the dessert at a dinner'.

* * *

**In other words, keep becoming successful…
but do stay interesting.**

187

"If you are not happy with 'what you have' then chances are that you will never be with what you will ever have".

***

Most of the people I meet are just plain 'restless' – restless to reach somewhere…achieve something… match someone. They have a perfect idea of their imperfection. They are sure that 'who and where they presently are' is not good; that that 'illusory good' is somewhere out there… on the horizon.

And that, with an X amount of hard work and determination, one day they will reach there and will then live happily ever after. You know what! The problem is not that they are in a race. The problem is that…

***

…now, the race is inside them.

188

**"Comparison is the coincidental
curse of civilization".**

* * *

There are days when as you walk down the street, everyone you come across looks more happy, fit, smart or successful than you. It is because you pretty well know your mask…and also what it is masking. Deep down inside, you are aware of all your fallings and failings. Your vulnerabilities and shortcomings are disclosed to you in their entirety.

You know what weighs on your mind, what bothers you in your heart, and what makes you wake up in the middle of the night and then doesn't let you sleep for the rest of it. In short, you know what you don't have, what you have, and what you show that you have but don't have. That's why, in every sense of the currency, everybody on the street looks far better off than you…

* * *

**…And you know what! Interestingly…most of the people you have
crossed have also been thinking the same.**

189

**All relationships are
'two-way' streets.**

* * *

It is convenient to be in a relationship as long as you are getting something in it – attention… time… love… care. But then comes a phase when the other person is not in a position to give, and in turn requires all of that. And that's the litmus test for a relationship – "Will now the getter be able to turn into a giver"?

Well, the most difficult thing in life is to bear the shift of spotlight elsewhere. Yes! Importance has a weird way to make a person hungry for more. However, in lasting relationships, partners have to be ready to alternately hold the torch and let the other person receive the shine. And that's where most relationships fail – because usually, one of the two is too addicted to 'shining'.

* * *

**All healthy relationships are about 'give and take'.
The only thing is to realize…'when to do what'.**

190

**Confidence is nothing but respect earned in one's own eyes
by fulfilling promises made to oneself.**

* * *

Over the years, I have seen best of the people literally wasting themselves because they were not loyal to the choices they made. And it is equally true for studies, work or relationships. Yes, it is important to stay the course even with reluctance or disinterest.

Well! As humans, we may have infinite potential but the problem is that we have finite time. And that makes the strongest case for discipline. And it is natural to get distracted or disillusioned, so even if you are finding it hard to stay the course, try to stay around it or bring it to a logical end. Don't just jump off the ship. As I put it "Sprint… run… walk…or crawl, make sure that direction remains the same".

* * *

**Such subtle messages to oneself create
'personality' inside person …one brick at a time.**

191

**As we sat in silence, she murmured
"Why, at times, life gives so much pain…?"**

* * *

I have always believed that the basic purpose of pain is to 'bring one's attention towards what needs to be changed. Yes, it is not a punishment …it is a signal. It arises to help us find what is amiss or missing, and not to make us suffer by getting lost in it.

So the greatest disservice to it is to treat it symptomatically, without delving into it. As it is not for nothing that sometimes it is intense… sometimes persisting…sometimes recurring. It has types; and each type has its own texture that has to be understood in finer details. From these details emerges the pain's purpose.

* * *

**Pain speaks. Listen to what it is saying and
then…do something about it.**

192

She asked "Why so happens that people are not there when I need them the most?" I said…"Because that is how it is meant to be".

* * *

While going through a difficult phase or after it, the worst thing you can do is to become cynical… to blame people for not being there… or to not forgive them for turning their backs on you. Because by doing so, you…miss the whole point. See it this way. A phase can qualify as a difficult phase only when you have to face it head-on, alone, and right there 'in your face'; with no one guarding you. After all, if there would be people protecting you then how would 'you' feel the heat?

Alas! Most people don't understand this. That's why they go through such phases and yet do not derive the value which is there for the taking. And the reason is that they direct their attention more to 'when who behaved how' rather than on 'why what happened'. What a waste!

* * *

The fact is that "your destiny delivers its most important messages in your loneliness". Don't shoot the messengers. Focus on the message.

193

**"In life, what matters the most is…
to remember what matters".**

* * *

There are people who like me. There are people who dislike me. There are people who used to like me and now tend to dislike me. There are people who used to dislike me and have begun to like me. There are people who think I am good. There are people who think I pretend to be good. There are people who are still evaluating me. There are people who don't even find me worth the effort.

And among all these there is a person who I have spotted around me for all these years. He is always present wherever I am – in all my situations…in all my circumstances – silently observing every thought and act of mine. He doesn't judge me. He doesn't categorize me. He doesn't even comment or remark. In fact, I have always got a feeling that probably he knows me beyond all the perceptions. And, all he seems to be interested in is whether I am continuously 'moving on' or not…

* * *

That person is…'me'

194

**Mind likes to chase a promised happiness
at the cost of the available one.**

* * *

If you taste a good dish then relish it…don't wait for a loved one to make it for you. If you find four happy faces around you then enjoy their company as if they are your family…don't wait to get back home to be happy. If you can rent a ride in your dream car then do so… don't give yourself a deadline to own it.

Happiness is a fleeting game of hormones, so it is idiotic to search for a perpetual one. Don't try to cook it through a recipe, have a heart like a monk's bowl and let destiny choose a time, a place and a person to bestow you with it.

* * *

**And when the bowl gets something, dance like a Sufi
…don't evaluate like an accountant.**

195

There is something about 'Goodness'
– about simple plain old-fashioned goodness.

❋ ❋ ❋

I know what you are thinking…that in today's frantic and factual life, it doesn't 'count for' much…that every day as each one of us walks downtown, there are far more important qualities required. To be liked, you need attractiveness. To be remembered, you need stylishness. To spot opportunities, you need alertness. To showcase self, you need aggressiveness. To stump competition, you need craftiness. To get ahead, you need smartness. To stay ahead, you need cleverness. And to change the game, you need shrewdness…

Boy!! It does take a lot to survive downtown. But, you know what! As you drive back, with all the glow-signs behind you, when you enter your home, then, to smile for no reason as you comb in front of the washbasin mirror, and to like the man you see there, all you need is basic deep-rooted Goodness…

❋ ❋ ❋

…the satisfaction that during the day, at no point did you forget that… your 'soul was not up for sale'.

196

Someone asked me the other day... "Why does 'being in love' feel so good"? I replied "Because of a simple but rare privilege it allows..."

* * *

You might ask "What privilege?"! Well, let me explain. If, in general, you list down things that give you pleasure or peace – be it looking at the moon, basking in the sun, dining in candlelight, riding a bike, sitting on a roller-coaster, dancing in a disc, smoking a cigarette, sipping a drink, gambling in a casino, watching a movie, playing a sport, going on a vacation, enjoying a shopping-experience, listening to a song, playing a guitar or even reading this post on my blog; then in any case, actually all you are looking for is just a way to...'be in this moment'.

Yes, all the above activities are merely creation of apparatus to facilitate that one thing. That's what you want; and honestly, that's all you need...to be happy. And for precisely the same reason being in love feels so good...When you are looking in eyes, holding hands, whispering in ears, touching face softly, running fingers through hair, feeling the warmth of each other's breath, coddling gently, hugging tightly, kissing with your eyes closed, or 'becoming One' ... in each of the cases, you are right there...in the moment.

* * *

**Yes, love feels good, not for what you do in it,
but for what it does for you.**

197

When it comes to the matters of heart…
"Everything takes a new dimension".

* * *

It is strange yet true that…in relationships, you mostly remember the things you had planned but never did, and others mostly remember the things that you did but never planned. They remember a word you had said, a smile that you had smiled, a look of admiration in your eyes, a pat on the shoulder, an instance when you had opened the door for them…

…a couplet you had quoted, an envelope on whose back you had written something, a spontaneous half-hug, a pen you never took back, an impromptu jig you broke into, or a moment of silence that you shared. Yes…! They remember little things. And it's because…

* * *

…in the realm of relationships,
"little things are… BIG things".

198

A relationship's real value manifests not in what it is to you, but in…what it does to you.

* * *

When it comes to long-term relationship, rather than choosing someone who can give love to your heart, choose someone who can give 'balance' to your life. The logic is a pretty simple one. Lasting happiness doesn't come in the form of excitement; it comes in the form of equilibrium. That's why, it is better to be with someone who can 'anchor' you, and give you deep roots to hold the structure of your life.

And yes, then it is important for you to play the same role in the other person's life. Well, such mutuality creates a synergy that helps both the persons grow. And then rather than being a high-maintenance machine, the relationship actually becomes the mechanic of your life.

* * *

Oh! But remember, the mechanic does ask for service charges.

199

**In most situations of life…"Being patient is
exactly what the doctor orders".**

* * *

Yes, it is amazing to discover that the solution of almost all problems
of life is the same – patience.

It combines with effort to form persistence…it combines with
acceptance to form tolerance…it combines with innocence to form
faith… it combines with vision to form focus… it combines with
resolve to form discipline… it combines with optimism to form
hope…

* * *

**…and it combines with your *decisions*
to form… your 'destiny'.**

200

<hr>

**In life, difficulties don't rip people apart,
it's the despondence.**

* * *

There are times when a person finds himself into a whirlwind of tough-times. And in such phases, things tend to go wrong in a heap. One thing leads to another and life hard-presses from multiple sides, with no respite. In fact, such relentless is the onslaught that the person is completely overwhelmed by the circumstances and feels that there is nothing to look forward to.

In such times, the only possibility of redemption lies in hope – hope that there is light at the end of the tunnel, that the good-times are just around the corner, that the person's best is ahead of them…yet to come, that a better and brighter tomorrow is waiting ahead. Well, this sense of hope doesn't reduce the weight on one's shoulders, but it increases the strength of the shoulders. And often, that's all it takes to start a turnaround.

* * *

**When you meet people, give them the gift of hope.
More people need it than you think.**

201

**People plan their wardrobes more meticulously
than they plan their life.**

❊ ❊ ❊

I am a strong proponent of not over-planning one's life, and I have also been a regular witness of what they call "Man proposes, God disposes". However, 'taking life as it comes' cannot be an excuse for not planning one's life. Let's not misuse philosophy to cover our negligence, reluctance, casualness or laziness. Don't get me wrong. I respect that life is uncertain, complex and ambiguous; and no one can guarantee what will happen next.

But that's precisely why we should plan the only thing we have a control on – our own actions. We can't simply solve immediate issues and start avoiding big-picture questions. It's neither meditative nor Zen. It is called escapism or 'running away from what you can't handle'. So, start observing what you are doing, begin to extrapolate what it will lead to, assess how far it is from what you want, and take corrective actions to prevent.

❊ ❊ ❊

**Do it all, even with
limited or varying success.**

202

**Some people have a knack for finding reasons to be sad;
that too consistently.**

* * *

By virtue of the nature of my work, many people trust me with their problems and trust me for a solution. I respect that trust immensely and do my absolute best to see a problem from that person's perspective – because only then can you visualize the perceived magnitude and feel the resultant suffering. Yes, at times life can be really cruel and world can be a very lonely place. However, every now and then, there are some people who simply amaze me with their ability to generate problems for themselves.

These people are fit and fine by most standards, and still are hell bent on being in a problem. And you would be amazed to understand the underlying motives to do so. They do so for two major reasons: it feeds their egos by helping them feel a pseudo sense of self-importance and it relieves them of going through the grill of "sweating it out" out there in the world. Yup! They devise problems to buy convenience.

* * *

**Why blame them? The truth is that all of us are prone to do so.
So keep checking.**

203

**Sometimes the best thing you can do for
someone dear is to simply "wait".**

* * *

He is one of my closest friends, and there is a development in his life that he has not shared with even his closest people. It's not that he doesn't want to share. He has been looking for reasons to meet me or talk to me. And often he mentions it and then he stops awkwardly or fidgets or stammers or simply changes the topic. The interesting part is that I already know what he wants to share. So when one of my loved ones asked me "Why don't you directly ask him about it or tell him that you already know"? I said "No, I will wait".

So why am I waiting? The reason is a deeper one. Well, even in our closest relationships, we protect our self-image – our perception in our own eyes vis-à-vis the other. That's why, when we want to expose our vulnerabilities, we want to do it in a way that still keeps our dignity intact. Even when we are full with emotions to the brim, we still look for the right coordinates of time and place to share. So I am letting him decide those coordinates, so that eventually when we will have that conversation, he won't regret.

* * *

**After all, real relationships are the ones in which we feel good even
after telling something 'not so good' about us.**

204

**When a woman smiles at a man, often it only means
"you are interesting" and not "she is interested".**

* * *

A characteristic problem with most (not all) men is that they try to read a tad too much. At times, a gesture conveying "I like you" can only mean "I like you" and doesn't necessarily translate into "there is a spark" or "would like to see you again" or "stay in touch" or "be around" or "there is more to it" or "you never know".

And even "I like you" doesn't mean "I will like you forever". It only means "I like you right now, for time being, for a specific reason, in a particular context, in the mood I am in, till I change my mind". But the issue is that at times, such intricate feelings are too complicated for some binary-thinking men. And they are only too happily eager to spot an illusory thing they are searching for – a cue…a clue…a hint. Well, what they don't understand is that at times…

* * *

**… it is good to simply smile back
at a smile, and move on.**

205

**More often than not, you will have
one of the four types of people in your life.**

* * *

First would be the people who will be happy in your happy times and neutral in your sad times. They are fair-weather companions – they will celebrate with you, but won't go out of the way to be around when the chips are down. Second would be the people who will be neutral in your happy times and sad in your sad times. They are bad-weather companions – they will be there when chips are down, but won't be around to raise a toast or give high-fives.

Third would be the people who will be sad in your happy times and happy in your sad times. They are your usual pseudo-companions – they will avoid letting you know that they are of this type, but you will realize it sooner or later. Then there would be a fourth type – the people who will be happy in your happy times and sad in your sad times. These are the people who you can call genuinely your own. This type is rare, special, and now close to extinction.

* * *

**If you have someone belonging to this last type then reciprocate.
That's when you will realize how tough it is to be one.**

206

**In life, most people never
admit their flaws.**

* * *

Some of these people were never told about their flaws so they think they never had them. It was probably because people around them were too doting, too considerate or too busy to mention them; or for that matter, possibly people around them also had the same flaws. Some of these people deliberately avoid looking at their flaws because that makes them feel low and nervous. So they adopt a defense-mechanism of denial. This saves them from any emotional dejection, and also from any mental discomfort of working towards correcting the flaws.

Some of these people name their flaws as their style. As a result, they develop an arrogant confidence about themselves. Consequently, people around them start getting intimidated and begin to accommodate. This lets these people believe that in life there is nothing like flaws. Well, whichever is the case, the common outcome is that these people, owing to the flaws they are blind to, are never able to unleash their full potential or establish meaningful connections. What a pity! These people fail to realize that…

* * *

**…"While seeing wounds in mirror, you can't apply Band-Aid
on the mirror and then hope to heal".**

207

**Not all relationships that work,
work for both partners.**

* * *

There are times when, to make a relationship work, one of the two has redefined his priorities, has learnt to stay quiet, or has reduced her expectations from the relationship, or has changed himself completely. And this has yielded results, because at least on surface, everything has stabilized. But it is a façade. Beneath the surface, things will only get complicated with time. The person who has adjusted will continue to feel a sense of dissatisfaction, paranoia, betrayal, and even vengeance.

And it all will affect the long-term health of the relationship. At one point in future, this gradual corrosion will begin to show. It will get manifested in that person's physical health, mental fitness and emotional condition. It will start with little changes in behavior and will end up engulfing not only both the individuals but also the relationship. And from there, there is no coming back.

* * *

**Relationships are meant to create synergy.
Alas, some end up only sapping it.**

208

**You have to work on a relationship
to make it work.**

* * *

Ideally, only two equally committed people can make a relationship work. However, in reality, at any given point of time, the commitment levels of two persons in a relationship can never be equal. It is because while they share a part of their lives with each other, there are other parts of their respective lives that they have to deal-with on their own. Those parts cannot be shared. At best, one can talk about them or take temporary help, but at the end of the day, one has to face it alone.

Now, what it means for a relationship is that one of the two will always have something else on his or her mind – some insecurities, worries, priorities, deadlines or concerns. That's when the other one has to play his or her part. He or she has to wait without cribbing, support without advising, care without clinging, forgive without mentioning, bear without sentimentalizing, or discuss disagreements without playing a victim. Yes, more often than not, one of the two will find himself or herself doing this.

* * *

**And as long as both can take turns to play
this role well, the relationship works.**

209

**Do not expect sympathy for your sacrifices.
Newer versions of 'world' may not support these features.**

* * *

The biggest problem for most of us is that the world we were brought-up in and the world we are living in are very different. The virtues that were once celebrated are now no more in trend. But they have been installed so deeply into us that in spite of believing that we have rationalized our expectations, we haven't been able to let go of those old values in the book. We still are suckers for fairness and poetic justice. But the fact is that in many cases power beats truth… manipulation beats capability…greed beats conscience – and that too hands-down.

However, the problem is that though we know this happens, we still can't stomach it without a burp. Yes, though we pretend to shrug it off, we still go back home sad and sullen. So then what to do about this dissonance? Well, just remember… subscribing to old-world virtues is a choice you make. You could have opted to let go, but it was your choice to hold on to them. And every choice comes with consequences. So what's the use of goodness if it makes you frustrated or cynical?

* * *

**Well, when you choose a stand others don't embrace,
learn to accept the consequences with grace.**

210

**When you are away from home – in a different city –
then it's in the evening that you begin to miss home the most.**

* * *

As the sun starts to set on the horizon and darkness blends with
the streetlights, you feel a certain emptiness in your gut. There are
people everywhere, and yet you feel utter loneliness. The skyscrapers,
billboards and flyovers only add to that feeling of being lost. You miss
the familiar feel and fragrance of your home, and effortlessness with
which you blend in with the surroundings. And then you suddenly
feel an intense urge to go back to where you belong.

There is an impulse to simply pack-up and leave… to go back to your
own cozy place, in the company of your own people. But then you
get reminded of the number of kilometers in between, and you get
a sinking feeling in your heart. You bite your lip, and breathe deeply
to counter that feeling of vertigo. Eventually, you surrender to the
inevitability of separation from nest that each boy and girl has to go
through, in order to become a man and woman.

* * *

**'Growing up' gives you many privileges. But it takes away one – to
stay the calf who invariably followed the cows back home.**

211

**It is immensely painful when someone close
doesn't understand how you are feeling.**

* * *

Though there are many people in your life who don't empathize
with you in your low phase but you don't feel that bad. And then
there is one person whose emotional-unavailability makes you feel
lonely – probably because you expected that person to instinctively
understand the unsaid. Now, in order to bring that person's attention,
you begin to do all sorts of things – you either behave oddly or stop
talking or speak indirectly or avoid completely or create a scene
needlessly or even go directly and plead.

Well, you eventually succeed in catching the eyeballs. But in the
process, you lose your valuable self-esteem. So you start to feel even
worse. Already hurt, now you are also devoid of the saving grace that
you had. As a result, you now feel weak and worthless. And that's
when the real suffering starts. It's amazing how, when you are hurt,
your close ones can either heal you for better or…

* * *

…hurt you for worse.

212

**Don't expect life to be fair. It is just the way it is.
And it has always been this way, even when you were not here.**

* * *

The best description of 'immune system' I have come across is that
"to see what immune system is, just see what happens to a dead
body". Yes, once you die, it only takes a few weeks for bacteria,
microbes, parasites etc. to feast on your body until all that is left is
a skeleton. And it happens because your immune system has shut
down, and the door is left wide open.

Something similar happens even in life. When you are weak and
fragile, you suddenly see things around you changing in unexpected
ways. People around you start speaking with a different tone, pitch
and volume. The whole treatment changes – you are taken advantage
of, or even worse, for granted. You discover that you are lonely and
have suddenly become everyone's target. Actually you are wrong. You
have not become a target now. You were always a target. It's just that
now you are a soft one.

* * *

**And, don't you know that…
"It is easy to chew a soft thing".**

213

**Neither your best defines you
nor your worst.**

* * *

All they help identify is your range, but not your nature. Thus, a mistake you committed, a relationship you messed up, an exam you flunked, a decision that backfired, or an opportunity you missed cannot define you. Still a lot of people tend to build their perception of themselves around that one-odd event or phase. Well, while it is okay for someone else to use them to form your image, it is a grave error to let that define your identity in your own eyes.

Peaks – whether negative or positive – are not representative. In fact they are often misleading. As a result, I often come across people who have either not forgiven themselves for something in the past or are still under a hangover of a bygone glory. They continue to drag a tomb or an emblem in their subconscious that weighs them down heavily as they walk in present…towards future. Eventually, it affects everything about their life – the pace, the direction and the motivation.

* * *

Let's grow out of childhood fascination for angels and demons, and stay humans – flawed, random and full of contradictions.

214

You prove a mistake a mistake only in two cases – when you take what you should miss, and when you miss what you should take.

* * *

What I mean by taking what you should miss is that after a mistake, people focus too much on how they are feeling about it. They typically roll themselves in self-worn guilt and flaunt a long face. While this reaction is a natural one initially, people deliberately elongate it either to prove their sincerity to those around them or to feed their own ego. It's the junk that most people hold onto uselessly.

And what I mean by missing what you should take is that after a mistake, people lose an opportunity to take valuable observations – why it happened, when it all went out of their hands, what they should do now, where does it all lead to or how they can salvage what still can be. Yes, every mistake should be followed by a heightened awareness and sharpened sense of objectivity.

* * *

The fact is that "More than the mistake, it is what people do after it that costs more".

215

"He was a liar; he had said that I am his life"
...she said while sobbing uncontrollably.

* * *

Well when, in love, a man says "I can't live without you" or a woman says "You are my world" then normally none of them is lying. Actually, they really mean it. They feel exactly that way in that moment. So, they are not cheating, they are simply feeling something out of ordinary, which unfortunately, can't be felt for ever.

The truth is that any extreme emotion, be it love or hate, can't arise unless a person exaggerates a certain feature of the other person. Yes, that exaggeration is essential to extreme emotions. And you can't blame people for seeing things out of proportions; it just doesn't qualify as deception. So, if you had heard those words from someone for whom now you seem to be a nonentity, then don't think that you fell for a lie. It's just that...

* * *

...it was an 'Absolute truth', in that
transient moment of ever-changing life.

216

Isn't it strange that "It is hard to establish your innocence if you don't shout, don't emote, or aren't the first one to tell the tale".

❋ ❋ ❋

Because by then, the impressions are all made, on the basis of the version that reached the ears first. Now, that is taken as the original, and yours is measured against it. You are no more the accepted, you are the challenger. Now you can't just tell…you have to prove.

So now you have to make your version more convincing and make yourself more persuasive. You have to weave the story in such a manner that it wins over the audience. You keep setting the right mood, mode and tone to the whole act, until it becomes a foolproof manuscript…

❋ ❋ ❋

…only to realize that it is
no more…authentic.

217

There are some people in your life that you bear because they are important to people who are important to you.

* * *

It is a thankless pursuit, and it feels as if all the time and the energy that you have to put-in to somehow bear the entire charade is a sort of fixed cost that you are supposed to incur irrespective of what you are getting out of it. Well, all said, it does get unbearable at times, and you want to break away from the whole drudgery.

But then you have to remind yourself that this short-term inconvenience has to be borne to sustain the overall stability of your life. Whether you see it as a sacrifice or a compromise, it is there to be made. And you have to muster all the mental and emotional guts within yourself to go through the grind every time it reappears. So you ought to learn to suffer fools. They are inevitable part of life.

* * *

And well, if you still find it difficult… just remind yourself that someone must be bearing you for precisely the same reason.

218

**Almost everyone sensitive figures out that…
"World can be quite a lonely place at times".**

***

There may be people sitting inches away from you and still you feel an invisible wall in between, through which, although you can listen to the words and look at the smiles, no warmth reaches your heart and no vibes touch your soul. As if something that nourishes togetherness isn't quite there…the secret recipe that characterizes the real connection.

It all feels superficial and akin to a role-play. And somewhere in the gut, you feel a void, a vacuum that is engulfing your whole system. It is sad because it feels real, and scary. Well, all you hope for is that something is not irreparably wrong in your head. And to top it all, you can't even tell someone that you are lonely, because, given the apparatus around you, you don't technically qualify as one.

***

Someone said it right – "Life is a comedy for those who think, and tragedy for those who feel".

219

**What is at the base of a relationship
decides what it will face.**

* * *

Breakups take place in the relationships of all shapes and sizes, but interestingly, one thing that is common among most of them is the reason behind the breakup – dissimilar expectations. Yes, if you pick a sample of relationships that hit the rocks, the two persons must have been looking for two different things.

While one would have wanted an hourly update interaction, the other would have wanted no strings attached type; while one would have wanted physical intimacy, the other would have wanted tender talks; while one would have seen it as a part of life, the other would have seen it as life; and the best of all…while one would have wanted commitment, the other would have wanted more time to understand each other.

* * *

**The key to a successful relationship is
similar expectations. Rest all takes care of itself.**

220

The species that is at most risk of extinction is not tigers or turtles, it is listeners.

* * *

… Someone who can sit in front of you without a rush to be somewhere else, a tendency to check on a gadget, an attempt to look over your shoulder, a temptation to glance at the watch, or a restlessness to interject at a pause.

… and someone who isn't busy forming an opinion, reaching a conclusion or preparing a reply. Well, you might ask that then what the use of such listening is. Okay! Then let me ask something. How about doing something not for utility, but simply for…

* * *

…Sensitivity.

221

At times, all you want from life is
"No high, no low, just a gentle flow".

* * *

So habituated have we become to the addiction of a happening life that we forget the sheer bliss of a life just flowing effortlessly. Some moments when the mind is neither positive nor negative, but is just staying in neutrality… just the usual heartbeat and belly breathing.

… just blending with surroundings and complete absorption into what is going on… surrendering to the vastness of life without intellectualizing or sentimentalizing. In short, when we aren't hurried into meaningless pursuit of finding a meaning to life.

* * *

Just like going on a long drive.
No destination…no deadlines.

222

**Any creation in life starts with a moment of passion,
but then requires movement with patience.**

❋ ❋ ❋

It is a fact of nature that while the fruit-bearing branches get all the spotlight, below the ground lay roots that nurture those branches… doing an unglamorous job, deep-down, in a muddy terrain. And through this, the nature reveals one of its biggest secrets.

Whenever you want to build anything worthwhile – relationship, career, or even self – it is vital to remember that passion is a catalyst. It should come at opportune times and then give way to its old-fashioned mate patience, which then takes up the drudgery of mashing up potatoes, singing lullabies and changing diapers for the brainchild that was born in a moment of passion.

❋ ❋ ❋

**Well, with passion, only conception happens.
For creation to take place…patience has to parent it.**

223

**The greatest rule of life is
"Life only processes the inputs it gets".**

❀ ❀ ❀

Yes, except some accidental occurrences, 99% of our sufferings are direct or indirect results of the seeds we had sown at some point of time in our life. It is just that the time-gap between the sowing of seeds and appearance of crop is so long that we are not able to identify the connection. But truth remains that the crops we reap are a result of the seeds we had sown.

In fact, it would be logical to say that the only test of which seeds were sown is the crop we get. Rest all is merely an intellectual ritual. And seeds have nothing to do with what you were thinking at the time of sowing. You might be thinking that you are sowing seeds of bliss, but if the seeds are that of pain then the crop will reflect that. Results aren't born out of the thoughts we think, they come out of the acts we act.

❀ ❀ ❀

Thus…no matter how much you disown…your life only comes out of the seeds you have sown…the ones of your own.

224

**In almost every family, there seems to be
a wise and…an otherwise.**

* * *

Wise is responsible for everything, because he is…well…'responsible'.
Whatever the wise does, he is expected to do it more and better; as he
has to also fill in for the irresponsibleness of the otherwise. So, while
otherwise gets away with tens of mistakes, the wise is kept reminded
of his one. And still, wise is supposed to forgive otherwise and adjust
to accommodate. And thus, otherwise keeps spilling it all, and the
wise is left mopping it up.

No one takes care of wise because everyone thinks he can take care
of himself. So, wise doesn't shout or cry. He simply bottles it up and
suffers. He breaks inside to keep the facade intact, and has to work
ceaselessly to live up to expectations that he seems to be eternally falling
short of. Still, his remains an ignored tale of silent sacrificing. Well,
every night, while the otherwise is snoring his way to a carefree sleep…

* * *

**…the wise keeps staring the roof, bearing in his beings…
the burden of wisdom.**

225

When you are in love, every sacrifice feels like a pleasure…and when you fall out of love, every adjustment seems like a sacrifice.

* * *

"Giving" is the only surest sign of being in love, and estimation of what you got is the surest symptom of falling out of it. This holds true for every domain in life. Oh! Let me explain how? Well, when you are in love, the center of your life shifts outside you. And then one day, it returns. And then starts the calculation – of what is gained and what is lost.

And interestingly, eventually everybody finds out that overall he made a loss. So then he thinks that he has found the reason why the relationship did not work – because he got very less and gave a lot more. Well, what he forgets is that, all that while when he was happy in the relationship, he was actually making losses.

* * *

Yes, it's the calculation that caused the problem.

226

If an emotion comes and goes then its reason is outside you, but whenever an emotion stays for long then its reason lies inside you.

* * *

Anger can be of two types. First type is the one that comes intensely and goes. It is normally directed towards events, and it is only just a side-effect that a part of it spills over to the people involved in that event. Second type is the one that stays. It boils inside at a temperature that lets you neither vent it out nor gulp it. Such anger is normally directed towards people.

But what helps it stay inside? It's 'you'. You provide it the energy needed for its sustenance. And you do it because such anger constantly pumps your ego and after some time, you unknowingly start enjoying the perk of the sense of importance that comes with it. And then begins the masochistic pleasure of fueling the very fire that is burning you. The fact is that nothing is more pleasurable than a simmering anger inside. It makes you feel alive, strong and an object of significance.

* * *

So, stop blaming others for what you are going through; because it began as a chance but…has now turned into a choice.

227

Strip people off their success, and what remains is their real self-esteem.

* * *

He came back home and everyone was waiting in the dining room. He winked at her romantically and gave a half hug to them, looking in their eyes with all the affection. Then he made a dash to the washroom, came back in a jiffy, and there he was at the dining table, regaling them with his anecdotes of their choice, and squeezing her hand softly while passing the dish. They ate their favorite dessert glued together to the primetime comedy, and then followed a drive in the silence of the day-long shrieking by-lanes.

As they were coming back, she suddenly got reminded of something and asked *"Oh! And how did that crucial meeting go?"* He looked in the rear mirror at those calm faces that dozed off on the backseat, and said *"We lost that deal"*. She put her hand on his hand and a minute's silence passed by. Then she said *"Is it a good enough reason to miss tomorrow's movie?"* Well, he looked at her…

* * *

…and both said "Nah"!

228

I was upset…because she was upset.

❋ ❋ ❋

…but seeing me upset, she got more upset…which made me upset
even more. And now it was a self-sustaining chain.

So I paused. Breathed deeply…and then I smiled, to which she didn't.
I still smiled, this time she attempted a fake one…which made me
laugh, to which she smiled. And it was again a self-sustaining chain.

❋ ❋ ❋

**In relationships, it's not about who was wrong,
it is about what's the right thing to do, now.**

229

**Relationships have a far-reaching impact
than mere emotional transactions.**

❁ ❁ ❁

Someone asked me the other day, "How can I know whether someone I am in a relationship with is right for me or not"? And my reply was "Just ask yourself if he or she helps you become a better person"! Yes, in any relationship, it is important to help the other person become a better person – a person with more restraint, greater resolve and faster resurgence. That's what separates relationships from mere affection or attachment.

You may ask "What if I am stuck in a relationship with a person who doesn't make me a better person" Hmm. It's a toughie. All I can say is what I usually tell people… "When everyone else fails you, it's time to test your own relationship with yourself". Yes, then keep helping yourself become a better person.

❁ ❁ ❁

**If you can't do it yourself,
you can't do it to others.**

230

Falling in love is a beautiful feeling…

❋ ❋ ❋

When you fall in love, making promises becomes easier. The words like 'always', 'forever', 'everything' are used in almost every other sentence. You give each other special names and devise your own unique ways to wish goodnights. You write long mails making commitments for eternity and press F5 every time you check your inbox…

…You discover that the phone is meant to be always kept nearby and is supposed to be locked by a password that now at least one person also knows. You talk in low husky voices at the most peak times and text 'miss you' so often that the phone mistakes it for your by-default template. And then, one day…a turning tide takes away all this with it.

❋ ❋ ❋

Well, it was the honeymoon phase of love. The real love is to quietly stand by someone's side…fulfilling all the promises you never made.

231

They are right when they say "Life is what keeps passing by while we are planning how to live it".

* * *

It was for a tad too many days in a row that I was doing a lot of things together. All of them were important but I was really missing that sense of directional connectivity I like to keep in what I do every day. And worse, the other day, I ended up with something that required documents, photocopies, waiting and then driving through the messy traffic to fetch more documents and their photocopies (not to forget…all of them attested).

While I was waiting…frustrated, irritable and thinking how much I wanted to get a life; suddenly, it dawned upon me that the life is happening here and now. True! Most of our life actually takes place between two such desired moments…overlooked by us, because we are too busy looking forward to the next such moment. Well, honestly speaking, even with my newly found wisdom, I still didn't enjoy what I went through that moment onward. But I surely came back less tired.

* * *

**"If I can't get my money back…then
let me take out the best from the ride".**

232

**He held his kid in his arms for the first time,
and lost all his rights.**

❋ ❋ ❋

Since then, everyone has ignored that he also gets bogged down by the weight of life, gets troubled by the residues of all negative he has to counter in everyday struggles, and gets tired convincing his heart to keep sacrificing what it wants; so that the greater-good prevails. Now, he is all the time busy controlling, balancing, providing and protecting…all for that kid who looks up to him.

And that kid seems to have forgotten forever that he is also a man. That how much he would sometime want to bang his fist on the table, shriek his heart out or hurl abuses in thin air. But here he is, caged in the notion of being perfect, forced to pose as a role-model; clenching his fists tight, biting his lips hard…all for that kid who is watching.

❋ ❋ ❋

**How much he *wishes* that kid could someday tell him…
"It's okay dad. You can let loose. I understand".**

233

**You may not be the reason of your sufferings…but
you got to be the reason for your revival.**

* * *

We always tend to glorify our struggles and undermine others'. It is ego's favorite game, because by doing it, we gain a certain sense of importance in our own eyes. We relish the feeling of being a martyr – the one forced by the villains of our life to go through a lot. But the fact is that everyone is battling with something…exorcising his own demons.

It's just that when we keep playing our stories in our minds we forget that they are told from only one angle – that of the protagonist. So, stop playing the old story in your mind and go out there to create a better one. Well, don't focus on what's lost, look at what's left and can still be gained. If you think you always got a rough deal from life, then now go to life and negotiate a better one.

* * *

**As they say "you can't go back and change the beginning…
but you can start now and choose a new end".**

234

**Our strengths are similar to each other's…
it's our weaknesses that set us apart.**

❋ ❋ ❋

Yes, you heard it right – "in our weaknesses lie the seeds of our uniqueness". Well, we have always been conditioned to shape ourselves as per the mold of perfect self created by the society. That mold contains only the qualities that are favorable to society as a whole and excludes all those that foster individuality. They called the latter ones 'weaknesses'.

So, watch your weaknesses in all their details, carefully maneuver them into your individuality, and continue to nurture them even in the wake of all the criticism. It would take time, yet when this process would be complete then you would see manifestation of the God's brushstrokes exclusive to you.

❋ ❋ ❋

**…and *hence* would begin a life that
you may call your own.**

235

**We segregate people, not because they can be…
but because then it is convenient for us.**

* * *

I have an amazing ability to be both wise and stupid. And I explore both these sides equally. In some contexts, I am absolutely senseless, sentimental, sluggish and even sleazy; and then in some others, I am immensely proper, poised, profound, and even near-perfect.

The most amusing moments for me are the ones when coincidentally I am in front of two persons who have been exposed to these two different facets of mine. And when both of them get to listen about each other's impression of me, one of them ends up inferring that I am wisely idiotic and the other lands up concluding that I am idiotically wise.

* * *

And there I am…smiling with conceit…because I can see that none of them is interested in knowing me, as they are busy defending what they know.

236

**The best treatment for hearts is not allopathy
or homeopathy. It is…empathy.**

* * *

It is almost extinct. When you share your pain with others then while
they are hearing you, they are actually busy comparing your pain
with their own. If it is less than theirs then they feel jealous, and if it is
more than theirs, they feel relieved. But in either case, their auto-tape
is on. At best, your pain works as a barometer for the state of their life.

So, next time when you share your pain with someone, do it
purely for the relief of getting an outlet and don't ruin that relief by
expecting others to feel it. Compassion is rare, don't expect it from
everyone. However, if you have a few who also lend their hearts when
they lend their ears, preserve them.

* * *

**And yes, next time, when someone shares his pain…
do try to keep your auto-tape off.**

237

Being modern is also about inventing
new devices to suffer.

✸ ✸ ✸

True! Look at us…we are all civilized people. Highly educated, well-dressed, properly groomed, socially savvy. We don't have to fight malnutrition, poverty, illiteracy, poor sanitation or gang-wars. Still…we suffer.

Our villains are inner –the expectations and the ambitions, the grudges and the regrets, the comparisons and the complexes, the insecurities and the distrust, and the angst and the restlessness.

✸ ✸ ✸

For us, happiness is no more a function of *what we have…*
it is about how we manage our emotions on what we don't have.

238

**In the matters of heart,
not everything makes complete sense.**

* * *

There are moments in life when all the witnesses and evidences are saying otherwise, yet a part of you says… "Go for it"! Shouldn't be surprising, as with all those years of conditioning, belief is no more an unconditional gift. It has to be earned after all the due-diligence has been done.

But even after the intelligence has announced its verdict, a tiny twirl in the gut keeps that plea alive. Probably, deep down inside, there is something that the heart knows, which the mind is too high- headed to register. So, if it doesn't cost you the bank, do take that leap of faith, because while others see it as illogical…

* * *

…you know it is…'Dil-logical'.

239

**In a finite life, no experience can last forever,
yet the change it brings…can.**

❋ ❋ ❋

There are phases in life when you simply run out of luck. Nothing seems to be going right and everything seems to be falling apart, brick by brick. It becomes a whirlwind where the harder you try, the worse it gets. And you are rendered utterly helpless. In such phases, people avoid feeling that helplessness by being optimistic, religious, fatalist, superstitious or even cynical. Such a waste of an opportunity!

Well! When you go through one such phase, simply surrender to the experience and flow with the flow. Feel that helplessness comprehensively, because it brings to you a realization that you were never the doer, but are at best…a participant.

❋ ❋ ❋

**With that realization, you would still try ever so harder
and yet…live far lighter.**

240

**Standing purposelessly in the balcony is
almost …meditative.**

* * *

As I stood there, with only a section of the road visible to me, I could
see all sorts of people passing by. Gradually it became a game of
sorts. I started looking forward to see who would enter next and then
would just witness the vehicle they took, the stuff they carried, the
words they spoke, gestures they made and how they interacted.

Well, life for each one of us is like our section of that eternal road.
People enter in that section because it came en-route. Thus, the
relevance lies if only we could let them take their journey through that
section without wishing someone hadn't come, stayed longer or would
never leave. That way, we would respect the reasons for which our
paths crossed, experience their presence without possessing it, and…

* * *

…most importantly, enjoy the…balcony-view.

241

They are right when they say "Love is a set of relatively-permanent emotions shared equally by two persons for mutual benefit and fulfillment".

* * *

No matter how much you deny, the fact is that you are the centre of your life. So in any relationship, your focus may be temporarily on the other person but sooner or later it shifts back on to yourself. And as you come back in the spotlight, you evaluate the relationship in terms of 'Return on Investment' and of course expect it to be high; which obviously can't be…because the other person expects the same.

Well, that's why, when relationships get messed up, it is usually not the relationship but one or both the persons getting messed up in their minds. So, the good news is that because it is all in your own mind so eventually only you can sort it out; which automatically translates into the bad news being that no matter how much you would love to blame the other person, the responsibility is on…you.

* * *

**In relationships, don't try to manage people…
try to manage your expectations from them.**

242

**No one has ever said "Why don't you understand?"
without being upset.**

* * *

Being misunderstood is probably one of the most discomforting things in life. Everyone is equally pained when they are misinterpreted, misquoted or mistaken. But why is it so? Well, we don't exist as real people but as images in people's minds. Our identity has less to do with who we are and more with what they think we are.

And being misunderstood is a reminder of this existential dependency. And when we fall victim to this dependency then we stand utterly helpless, frustrated on the inability of words in bridging the gap and dejected by the shallowness of all the means to connect.

* * *

**That's why, far more valuable than "I love you" or "I respect you"
is being told…"I understand".**

243

**Love should protect…
yet not deprive.**

❉ ❉ ❉

She said *"He's my love…he's alone and needs me, I must be there to reduce his struggle"*. I said *"Do support him while he is licking his wounds, but don't wish those wounds away…don't guard him from the fight. Let him struggle…and look at life in the eye, because that is what will make a man out of the boy"*.

I ended… *"So, I urge you to be there for him, BUT I warn you…DON'T you dare interfere in…the making of a man"*.

❉ ❉ ❉

**Love should do its job…and
let life do its own.**

244

When you break promises made to others, you lose reputation…
but when you break promises made to yourself, you lose
confidence.

* * *

Interestingly, when you resolve, then a part of your mind immediately starts revolting. The reason is simple, because both emerge from the same place – mind. So, what you need is not a resolution of what you want to do, rather, you need an awareness of why you do what you don't want to do or don't do what you want to do.

Let me explain. I have always believed that Geeta is all about symbolism. Arjun represents mind (mann) and Krishn represents intellect (vivek). And when Arjun loses confidence to fight, Krishn doesn't motivate him…he explains. He ensures that now when Arjun stands up, he doesn't operate through willpower of mind (mann)… but from the clarity of intellect (vivek).

* * *

Well, transformation doesn't occur by claiming fists,
it takes place from brooding chins.

245

When relationships hit rough patches and subsequently people patch up, all said, something isn't the same anymore.

* * *

A part of you dies – the innocent overconfidence in the concept of forever…the belief in ever after born out of deeply ingrained fairy-tales heard in cozy cushions on wintry nights during childhood. You discover the fragility and fallibility of the words 'never' and 'always'; and for the first time you don't cringe at the boring-aunt's advice of "be practical"…as now you know how she got this boring.

You are more strong now, more ready to accept the unacceptable, more willing to think the unthinkable. Now, you know – "Where movies end…life begins". Oh, but don't be cynical. All those fairy-tales were true. It is just that you have outgrown them by opting to explore what lies beyond them – the next stage of growing up.

* * *

**Don't worry, you will be fine soon…
even if it isn't fine anymore.**

246

They are right when they say "When you do everything on time then you have time for everything".

✳ ✳ ✳

I am no fan of handing over one's life to the hands of the clock and am also not a punctuality fanatic who closes the door on people's faces. I vouch for free will and endorse the liberty to live by an inner compass rather than by the watch on the wrist. Yet I am a firm believer in having an awareness of the passage of time.

It is important to have a sense of the apt timing, duration and frequency of every insignificant yet concrete act that you pursue. As, put together, they form the abstract concept called life. So I wouldn't want to be a horse with the blinders on. But I also wouldn't want to be a street-dog who lets his tendencies and temptations decide the course of his day.

✳ ✳ ✳

…I would be more comfortable being a human with the discretion to choose when to be what, and enough will-power to stand by his choice.

247

They are right when the say
"Someone's tragedy is someone's comedy".

* * *

In the veil of the concept of society, we have created an unnatural system binding individuals through a notion called humanity. Although it has been pushed into us through a consistent hammering of values, morals and ethics; yet the animal-ness inside us surfaces whenever one is alone or in a mob (individual accountability diminishes, thus one becomes as safe as 'alone').

In such unguarded moments, we are as individuals (as good and as bad) as animals – perfectly capable of doing everything that is prescribed to be avoided by humanity…seeing emotionless as a bystander, enjoying sadistically or even taking advantage.

* * *

It is only in one's worst moments does one realize the futility of having endlessly spent needless energy on maintaining the status of a social being.

248

**I hate waking up early but
love everything that follows.**

* * *

There is something surreal about early mornings. The world is closest to how it is meant to be…in creator's brushstrokes – silent, stable and subtle. The creation is just starting to take over, but the lord is still in charge. Everyone in the nature is awake, except us.

And that is so because, last night, we were up till late…watching TV for the sake of it, working on laptop, checking fbs, reading worn out papers, chatting idly, texting intermittently or nibbling and gulping casually. In other words, doing everything possible to stretch the day, way past it, in tune with our desire to squeeze each day, to extract the maximum from it.

* * *

**But then…it's not only about getting the most out of life,
but also to get the best out of it.**

249

**Our mind doesn't deal with people,
it deals with its perceptions of them.**

* * *

I knew he was in love with someone and would often talk about her. And when I met her, I could see why! She was gorgeous. But you know what? I somehow felt that it would not work out. The reasons were deeper. Well, everyone who is good isn't automatically good for you. She was always nice to him but ever since they had been together, he seemed more restless, hunched, insecure and distracted. Her presence wouldn't bring out the best in him.

And she was nowhere to be blamed for it. Rather it was his own mind that, while positioning the perception of her personality in his psyche, had stumbled upon some deep-laying point of reference into the darker recesses of his past and had activated some related complexes or insecurities. So, now she had become more of a trigger to an algorithm of a downward spiral in his mind. And when that happens, you know it will not remain hunky-dory.

* * *

Well, fulfillment in relationships is not a function of people's impressions, but that of their impact on you.

250

**Falling in love is effortless.
Staying in love takes a lot of effort.**

✽ ✽ ✽

When you fall in love, your focus is on features and not on flaws. As the passion recedes, flaws start showing up. What starts with an unconditional acceptance then becomes an effort to mold the person according to your tastes and temperament. But staying in love is an altogether different ball-game. It is about seeing the other person not in terms of features or flaws but in terms of features and flaws. Yes, it is about acceptance of unacceptable and un-mold-able.

Well, staying in love is a different game altogether. It requires acknowledgement of dynamic nature of a human, continuous exploration into each other's evolution, ongoing adjustment in priorities, timely juggling of roles, realigning of expectations, reassessing of other variables in life's equation, and continual foregoing and forgiving; and yes…all accompanied by bona-fide humor. Phew, a lot of effort!

✽ ✽ ✽

**But you know something!! Whatever requires effort…
is generally worth that effort.**

251

No one listens to what anyone says because each one of us is too busy figuring out what the other one actually wants to say.

* * *

Being born as humans, it seems as if we are destined to live in a constant struggle between who we are and what we have to look like. We hardly ever say exactly what we feel like saying. What our heart speaks out has to go through mind's numerous filters like occasion, custom, motive, priority and stakes. The real feeling is forced to choose from man-made vocabulary, a word which minimizes the risk and maximizes the return.

And in the midst of this diplomacy, all we say is a distant optimized version of what we felt originally. Well, in the name of society, we have created a suffocating arrangement which stifles our original selves and hands us over the masks which increase our acceptability while eroding our authenticity. Every day as we walk down the busy aisles of our respective worlds, all we play is a guessing game.

* * *

Say what you mean. It may cost you the masks but shall win you an easier breathing; and fewer but worthy people around.

252

**Personality isn't about your impression on people…
but your impact on them.**

❈ ❈ ❈

It is not about how good you are, it is about how good others are
in your presence. I have seen a lot of people who, in the name of
developing their personality, focus a tad too much on themselves.
They think it's about being attractive in looks, articulate with words
and aristocratic at conduct. Well, it's fine if it all happens, but trivial
if chased.

Personality is not to be in the spotlight, but to hold it so that others
are able to see themselves better. It is not to hog the limelight…but to
share the screen-space. It is not just about being the best, but also to
bring out the best in others. And well, better if that impact becomes
an influence, felt beyond your presence.

❈ ❈ ❈

Yup! Pass on the torch.

253

Good people suffer because they are
mature enough to accommodate.

* * *

Have you ever observed a careless bike-rider driving rashly on busy roads? You would find that more often than not he doesn't meet any accident, because all other people on the road adjust their course to let him have his way. Life isn't much different either. So-called bad guys cruise through stubbornly, because the so-called good ones sacrifice and compensate on their behalf. And then they become disillusioned, bitter or cynical; cursing their own goodness.

Well, it's important to be good, but equally important to not let it become your weakness. In other words, a practical heart is a sheer waste. Heart should always be innocent, but then one should also have a strong mind which can guard its innocence.

* * *

Be strong, assertive, intelligent and decisive...
to stay genuine, soft, giving and innocent.

254

People aren't your fantasies, they are real people.

❋ ❋ ❋

Someone who self-admittedly has looked up to me for quite a few years now, recently told me "I found you quite different from how I always thought you were". I smiled and said *"Good that you got to know yourself through me"*. By the looks of it, I could judge that my terse philosophical reply was an overhead transmission.

Let me explain. When you admire someone then you actually paint a self-satisfying image of that person, which is nothing but the portrayal of your own ideal self. So through him, you either project your un-manifested complexes or satiate your own unfulfilled desires. It's a kind of 'play' in which you are the storywriter, screenplay writer, director and editor; and the other person is just an actor.

❋ ❋ ❋

Well, I can't live up to someone's imagination…
I am too busy living my reality.

255

They say "In love two become one". Oops!
But then the result is two half people.

* * *

Many people use love as a pain-relieving spray, as a means to fill a
void inside them – a void caused by something at a far deeper level.
It is like a temporary solution to a persisting problem. Day in day
out they play the same game – again and again. They know that their
aloneness would trigger soul-searching and their shallowness and
hollowness would stare them in their face. So they would hook-up,
text, chat, call, talk, wait, fret, meet, or in short, do anything that can
keep them off their self.

For them, belonging to someone is a way to becoming something.
They use emotional and physical intimacy as a tool to establish their
identity. It is like holding on to a pole because you can't stand on your
own, and that's why then any unresponsiveness from the partner
reduces their self-esteem and a break-up hurts their self-worth…
beyond repair. As a result, what was meant to be a natural sharing
between two hearts brimming with their completeness becomes
an arrangement by two confused minds to help hide each other's
incompleteness.

* * *

Well, love is not meant for halves. It is meant for two…
who are too full to 'not share'.

256

**The peak of pain isn't a scream…
it is an utter silence.**

❋ ❋ ❋

It is a stony quietness born out of the lonely realization that no one is around to listen…that now no one is coming to hold you, understand or comfort…you don't find anyone close enough even to complain to…you don't even want to cry because you think that the last shreds of self-esteem that you have managed to hold on to would get washed away by it.

You are too far from yourself to connect to anything else…You can't even think – it's absolutely blank inside…you change TV-channels and stop at anything that can go on in background without trying to affect you…the same Ghazals you cried on don't even soothe you because you've got too hardened to be pierced…and you know that the only way to sleep is to tire out yourself completely. And you can't help it all, as for you, desensitization was a survival-strategy.

❋ ❋ ❋

**If you are going through such a phase then
get ready, finish your breakfast and go to work…it's a great healer.**

257

**Beginnings are beautiful
– pure and innocent.**

* * *

For instance, the first love. When you fall in love for the first time, it is just a nameless feeling…a floating delicate bubble. There is no physicality involved. For you, she isn't a body…she is a presence. To an extent that you don't even crave for her attention, you are happy just to get to see her. To know that she is sitting in the same classroom, travelling in the same bus or breathing in the same city makes you feel connected to her – enough to make you smile even when you are alone.

Same thing happens when you become an entrepreneur. It is like being in love – this time with a concept. There is no ambition to mint money…just a desire to create…a wish to see manifestation of an abstract idea into a reality. For you, every receipt is a token of trust that someone placed in your dream. You don't see employees as resources, you see them as companions. You don't plan to make it big…you just want to keep doing more of what you love to do. And then…you become successful, and start looking up to achievement and looking down upon joy.

* * *

**Well, success is like passion –
it makes you forget the romance.**

258

**Whether something is a cost or an investment
can only be decided by what it is incurred for.**

❋ ❋ ❋

In the name of being mature, we learn to bear more and demand less.
We think of less than what we desire…we settle for lesser than what
we deserve…we tolerate what we don't like… we follow what we don't
agree with…we accept everything we can adjust with…we expect
only what we can't live without.

Ask yourself what you are doing it for! Well, compromises are
justifiable only if there is something larger in the long-term view.
But if not, you better know that in an effort to assemble everything
outside, you yourself are disintegrating inside.

❋ ❋ ❋

**And nothing is worth at the cost of
the one who is paying it.**

259

**The most frequent, simple and effective advice
is to 'Move On'.**

* * *

Ever rode a bicycle? Well, the most peculiar thing about riding a bicycle is that you can't tell anyone how you do it. It's a secret that you only discover on the move. You discover that it is a continuous struggle between you and the gravitational force.

It is pulling you down all the time and the only way to not fall is to be on the move. Well, in bicycle, just as in life, you are your own motor. And yes, in case you have to stop, keep your feet firmly grounded.

* * *

**That's what separates
stopping from falling.**

260

**Pain has an extraordinary ability to shape
your personality in a way nothing else can.**

❊ ❊ ❊

In happiness, you open up…bursting at the seams…keen to share…
anxious to reach out; your whole focus is outwards…towards
"belonging". In pain, you are left alone…converging onto yourself…
ripe to introspect…compelled to review; your whole focus is
inwards…towards "becoming".

Well, pain may not be good for you…but is for your good. And
remember, it is not forever…it will soon start descending (unless
you are hell-bent on holding on to it). It's an opportunity created for
something more significant to happen. It is preparing soil for a seed
of self-renewal.

❊ ❊ ❊

**And in farming, when a seed is sown…everything around it
presses and pressurizes it harshly just to… break its heart. In other
words…'sprout'.**

261

Beyond one's shores lies one's liberation.

* * *

It's only while traveling that you discover your real self. You get introduced to your worst fears and your greatest assets, you come to know the tensile strength of your will and resistivity of your emotions, you explore the hidden treasures of humor inside you and tap into the imaginativeness you never knew you had. It teaches you patience. You learn that most problems are not to be solved; they simply dissolve if you let them.

You learn that your instincts are your best friends and your knowledge can be your greatest enemy. You grow both 'by choice' and also by the lack of it. But most importantly, it helps you realize that you are just a lesser-mortal, a tiny bubble on the vast sea of existence. Thus it makes you think what you really stand for, what your inner calling is and where you actually belong. So get your backpacks ready and move out…out in the sun…where life is waiting to teach you at the school called 'world'.

* * *

**Well, I promise it won't be comfortable…but then…
who said evolution is convenient.**

262

**There is a lot of difference between
aspiration and ambition.**

* * *

We all have an instinctive calling, woven into our basic nature…our original being. When any person, thing, place, act or idea matches it, then we feel a native desire inside. This desire is unadulterated…innocent…pure. It is not a want to possess or acquire, but a longing to belong to it. Now this desire can be seemingly for absolutely materialistic things like a person, car, house, place or work… and yet it is rooted spiritually, because it emerged from inside. This is called aspiration.

On the other hand, we all have a mind which has been programmed by our experiences, observations and interactions. This mind compares and competes…and gets titillated & seduced. Out of which, a cold-blooded craving for certain things gets produced. This is a sensuous delight, to have or prove. Now this desire can be seemingly for all the spiritual things like service, contribution, Nirvana or even God…yet it is rooted materialistically, because it got induced from outside. This is called ambition.

* * *

**Aspiration for a car is far more divine than ambition for God.
It's about authenticity. Yes, that's the word.**

263

"I wish I would have come in his life earlier. I don't like the fact that there was someone else in his life before me"…she said.

* * *

I see life as an assembly-Line and people as Work-In-Progress. We go through a lifelong process of evolution in which we pass through various steps and stages. At each step, someone has been deputed with an assigned task to chisel or shape us towards what we are ordained to become…eventually.

That's why your Ex (be it ex-lover, ex-friend or ex-employer) deserves immense respect and gratitude from you. More so, because the one you have in your life now as finished-goods was handled by those Exes as a raw material; the one you find loving and lovable is a result of processing-pain and learning cost borne by those Exes. They made what you own today.

* * *

Well, they wrongly say 'Someone somewhere is made for you'. The correct version is…"Someone somewhere is being made for you".

264

**There are phases in life when all you are doing is
"running around everywhere".**

❋ ❋ ❋

Things are pulling you in different directions. Clock governs your thoughts and schedule rules your moves. Hours after hours, you are just filling the slots of time with activity and more activity. Plans…people…promises…priorities – everything is stacked tightly. All is normal to the naked eye, but inside, you know that you aren't heading anywhere.

In the name of busyness, you are simply a part of messiness… neither creating value nor adding it. You can't figure out how you landed here, and are even more clueless about how to get out of it. It is such helplessness as if you are trapped in a traffic jam – where it is not your discretion that decides your move, but the rowdiness of road and the whims of others that call the shots.

❋ ❋ ❋

In such a phase, remember…you will survive the mess sooner or later, just don't let it mess you up.

265

**Expecting someone to understand your feelings
is the surest way to suffer.**

* * *

How we feel is a function of three variables – the situation we are in, the way we perceive it and our sensitivity-level. At best, someone can understand the first, but rest two are uniquely-personal to us. No amount of empathy or listening can bridge this gap completely. In our desperate attempts to make someone understand and our frustration on its futility, we forget the fact that "We all live together, but in different worlds". The worlds designed in a customized manner by and for each one of us.

This difference is a reality that we try to ignore, as it will introduce us to a scary realization…of our loneliness. We created social groupings at all levels – families, friends, clans, localities, communities, castes, religions, nations, continents – but we cannot deny this truth that eventually we are seven-something billion lonely people. Though the denial is by and large successful, every now and then the realization keeps coming back to us.

* * *

**And that's where lies…the
seed of human-suffering.**

266

**When we postpone pleasure,
we disrespect a blessing.**

* * *

Our obsession for planning has crept even into the matters of heart. Now, even to be happy, we wait for perfect opportunities – the perfect setting, ambiance, company and modes. We want to govern the whole experience, not realizing that we are not the benefactor…we are the beneficiary. There are innumerous people who are trying to create happiness or even buy it… only waiting still for it. It is so because it cannot be manufactured…it happens to you by the call of
the providence.

So if you are feeling that upsurge of energy originating from your gut, traveling through all your being, culminating as a glow on your face and leaving behind lips 'kissed wide open'…then you just got lucky. This blissful moment is a blessing from the angels up there. They must have been celebrating and a drop of nectar has got spilled out. That drop chose you, so respect this divine coincidence and relish it completely. It is not wisdom, it's sheer truth. Don't wait for certain occasions and valid reasons to be happy. If it is happening then live it to the fullest.

* * *

**This moment is not coming again…
as it is already on its way out.**

267

**Some days can suddenly make you
look so *ordinary*.**

* * *

You wake up with a heavy head, your toothbrush heads straight to gum, soap keeps slipping away, towel isn't its usual dry, comb gives up on your hair, keys are misplaced, beverage is too hot for the time available for it, you see a spot on shirt after you've worn the shoes, and your tongue is obsessed chasing the elusive remnant.

At work, you are at best mundane, your usual tact with people is missing, your words aren't falling in place, you are bumping into people on blind-corners, an unanswered greeting is bothering you inside, your schedule goes topsy-turvy, and a phone line is dead and a deadline is phoned.

* * *

**Such days help you realize that in making you look good,
there are more factors at work than…you.**

268

The root of most of the human problems is that when someone named us Human Race, we thought… race was a verb.

* * *

Why race? All records get broken and all bests get beaten… every absolute becomes relative and every philosophy becomes a hypothesis…all facts turn out to be perceptions and all 'ahead of times' become 'once upon a time'. Yes, such is the might of time and force of change. Still, we keep entertaining our arrogant ignorance. Well, that's the problem with being human-Race'.

I believe that rather than Human-Race, we should be called "Human-Jog". Waking up for ourselves…strolling at our pace… enjoying the view… sharing warmth with companions… bantering with friends… smiling even to strangers… running occasional playful-sprints… celebrating 'Win' irrespective of who won… halting to rest and relish…

* * *

and eventually…reaching the spot on the hill, from where… we have the best view…of our own SUN.

269

Sometimes, when you are coming back from a successful moment, you feel tiny restlessness in your heart.

* * *

They are right when they say "Success is Public...but Failure is Private". Amidst all the standing-applauses, house-full boards, pats on the back, warm hugs and star-struck faces...only you know what you had really set out to do and achieve.

You might receive all the compliments with grace...pay tributes in turn...pass on the glory to your worthy impetus...but inside you, a part of you is sulking, cringing and twitching...because it knows what you had indeed embarked upon.

* * *

**And as long as you stay true to that part...
you know you are on-track.**

270

**Every protégé only feels great until
they become your competition.**

* * *

Isn't it amazing! When someone says that we are good, we feel flattered…when he says that he would want to become as good as we are, we feel honored…when he eventually becomes as good as we are, we feel insecure…and if he becomes better than us, we feel jealous.

So what's the way out? Well, let's first keep getting better…till we reach our best…and then…redefine 'best'. And more importantly…

* * *

**… let's replenish our souls;
something is not quite right there.**

271

**The truth is that the first person we fall
in love with… is 'ourselves'.**

* * *

And since then, the life is nothing but a voyage to stay in love with
ourselves… Be it the place where we live, the work that we do or
the choices that we make, everything is secretly aimed at this only.
We choose friends who either 'like us' or 'are like us', we build
associations which help us get better without making us feel inferior,
and we create relationships which don't try to change us beyond
our comfort.

In a way, we keep loving people who help us love ourselves more. It is
not selfishness; it is simply the way we are. In fact, what is strange is
that we all know about this fundamental need of each one of us, and
still we don't respect it enough. So let's help people be in love with
themselves…without confusing them into believing that they are
flawless or manipulating them to serve our interests.

* * *

**Well, it's the latter half that makes
the former tougher.**

272

I wish we were like the kids in annual function of a primary school situated in some small town of India.

* * *

Clapping all the time (without any cringes)… touching both the feet (of all the people on the stage)…smiling ear-to-ear (without a reason, or desire of asking for one)… saying 'thank you' (looking straight in the eye)… cheering for each other (actually)… holding their certificates tight (with a pride people don't even hold a fat pay-cheque with)… looking at their tiny-trophies with curiosity (rather than conceit)… joining hands for prayer (with eyes closed)… listening to what people on stage are saying (without evaluating them).

Well, as we grow up, we gain the most respected virtue in the world – intelligence…at the cost of the most cherished possession of ours – innocence.

* * *

**Think about it without a cringe,
if you still can.**

273

Professionalism is all about balance.

* * *

Professionals are great proponents of neutrality; they are thorough practitioners of level-headedness. They don't have extreme likes and dislikes and they don't travel peaks…they live on means and medians. It doesn't mean that they are indecisive; it just means that they are unbiased. They don't work against anybody, they don't have time to nurse grudges and they never turn back to dig the graves of past.

As if they have learnt to press F5 button on their temperament-keyboard…never forgetting to get back to their senses after a heated meeting with a colleague, a scolding session in boss's den or an exit interview in which the person called them names. Experts at elasticity… toggling between two emotional states and walking on the thin thread between two entirely opposite demands of a dilemmatic situation…effortlessly.

* * *

Let's strive to be so. It's a worthy aim.

274

**There is always a good side to
a bad phase.**

❋ ❋ ❋

We all have gone through our share of grief and struggle. In such a phase you suddenly discover how lonely you are and how cosmetic every second thing around you is. And when that happens, it is so easy to get permanently cynical about everything.

But pain can also be pretty 'purifying'. It introduces you to your inadequacies, your vulnerabilities and your insignificance in the larger scheme of things. It helps you to test whatever you had always believed in. It helps you crosscheck your assumptions and verify your conclusions. It forces you to just bare it all in your own eyes. And in the end, it leaves you more grounded and more aware of your own self.

❋ ❋ ❋

**Pain gives you a new pair of eyes
to look at the world through.**

275

**Popularity is gained, fame is attained,
and reputation is established.**

* * *

World likes to typecast you… stereotype you… to fit you into its
pre-made categories because then it finds it easier to use you for its
benefit. For that, it lays out a trap. If you fall for it then you are caged
inside a cage that is beautiful and rewarding…and still a cage at best.
It is called "fame".

You may decide rather to stay close to your core – the one thing for
which you were actually here…you can sacrifice the temptation,
smile the bait away and deny the comfort and privileges which come
in exchange of the compromises you are asked to make. You choose
to aspire to be more of who you already are. It is called reputation.

* * *

**Well, they come intertwined and one can't decide their sequence.
All that matters is… "Knowing your order of preference".**

276

**In life, you can expect to meet these
three kinds of people.**

* * *

First would be absolute angels. Value them, or else you will lose them.
Second would be absolute scoundrels. Avoid them, or else they will end
up dragging you to their level and will beat you with their expertise.

Third would be half angels – half scoundrels (most of us belong here).
When they show their angelic side then beware of their scoundrel
side, or else you will end up getting ditched; and when they show
their scoundrel side then remember their angelic side, or else you will
end up distrusting everyone in your life.

* * *

**It is about that "smart trust",
with open curious eyes.**

277

**The thing about decision is that, although you make them,
the world owns the deployment.**

* * *

Well, life is nothing but "a set of sheer coincidences, shared between randomly-running entities". All that is happening is random…and we just feel a pseudo sense-of-control by locking ourselves into a chosen orbit (our attempt to bring predictability). Step out of that orbit and you will realize how arbitrary everything becomes (is).

All the time, we are living coincidences. We ignore 90% of them because they have neutral impact on us, we name the 5% of favorable impact as 'good luck' and the other 5% of unfavorable impact as 'bad luck'. But, in reality, there is nothing such as luck…it's all coincidental.

* * *

**Yup! It is our own attempt 'in vain'
to find an algorithm.**

278

**The world is simply a reflection of
what is going on within you.**

❋ ❋ ❋

As I drove to work in the morning, the world looked heavenly. Open
and vacant roads enjoying their solitude… smiling kids waving at
me from the back-glass of their school-bus… a vegetable-vendor's
children who are jubilant because he has offered them a drive on his
handcart…

…a boulevard with that special greenness which comes only after
the trees are bathed in gentle rains… foggy horizon with a hint of
mystical-shade of morning-orange…breeze flowing with mildness and
shyness of someone who has just come to know she is in love. Well, I
am lucky to have this kind of a path to work every morning, Isn't it?

❋ ❋ ❋

**Well, not really, it is just that I was in a good mood today,
because for all these days, I spotted none of these.**

279

If people use you, it proves that you are useful
and not useless.

* * *

Well, if left to ourselves, we would never stretch ourselves beyond our comfort. So these people, who have used us, have actually helped us discover our utility. They helped us find our limits by pushing us to them. The truth is…we learn more from what we have not chosen… as, by choice we would only choose what resembles us.

So if you are being used then don't complain…get used to it. Just take care that you aren't being exploited. But now the question is…how to decide whether you are being used or exploited? Well, the thumb-rule is…if you have been waking up feeling used for too many days in a row…this is it.

* * *

After all, it was okay being used…
but not feeling that way.

280

**I am not against guilt, my reservation is
against its extended version.**

* * *

Yes, all I disagree with is how it has gone beyond its utility to create more problems than it solves. I see so many people suffering in the name of it… people feeling guilt and getting inert, people making other people feel guilt to then exploit them, people staying feeling-guilty and destroying themselves…and what not!

Well, guilt was supposed to be a trigger… purposed to act as a reminder. It was meant to activate us and initiate us into a corrective action…it wanted us to be progressive…not regressive. So, when you feel regret about something…then forget the feeling…and now…do something about it.

* * *

**It's not about how you felt.
It's about what you did after it.**

281

**Chasing something can be a bigger thrill than
actually getting it.**

❊ ❊ ❊

Well, coming out of your comfort zone and being back to where
rubber meets the road is not really much comforting. A part of you
feels daunted, wanting to go back to the familiar terrain of your cozy
world, where you are the king of your roost…where people know you
by your nick-names…where your life runs via either your organizer
or the schedule on the board. In short…'your space'.

But you forget how you reached that so-called 'your space'. What
today you call 'yours' was also once alien to you, a part of the
wilderness that you always feared. So, in fact, nothing is really yours
except that very quest which brought you there.

❊ ❊ ❊

**So prepare to again be out there…
for testing the hypothesis.**

282

**Don't become a commodity, traded on the
perception-exchanges of the world.**

* * *

In life, we all have something – a venture, a project, a deal, an exam
or a relationship – to which we give our 'everything' and it still
doesn't work out in the end… leaving us wondering how to deal with
it. It is natural to feel that way, because if we don't have benchmarks
then how would we evaluate things? After all, we are accountable to
someone somewhere for everything. Isn't it? Well, that's where my
difference-of-opinion is.

I do agree that all of us are answerable to the world for our deeds,
but if the world has all the right to evaluate us by our results (the
destination) we should still reserve the right to evaluate ourselves also
in terms of our effort (the journey). So, it is important to accept the
world's definition of failure and get affected temporarily by it, yet not
letting it permanently change your definition of success.

* * *

**Reserve your right to feel successful, if you really feel
"you gave your best shot to it".**

283

**The most painful feeling
in life is helplessness.**

❊ ❊ ❊

It is not pleasant when you see your ideals fail...when all you wanted
to pursue was excellence, yet what you have ended up with is average-
ness around...when the values that you had once sown have been
uprooted clinically...and when the same people who had once
partnered your dream have joined the conspiracy of its substandard-
version. All this leaves you with a sense of hopelessness –a feeling
that you are a failure...that you have succumbed to the ecosystem
of mediocrity...that you are the odd-one-out in your own clan...a
refugee in your own homeland. You feel...betrayed.

BUT then...you start getting the hang of it. You realize that this is
exactly what the cynics of the world wanted - to pull you down when
they could not push themselves up...to make you feel ashamed of
your own idealism because it wasn't easy on them... to declare you
a *schizophrenic* because they could not see the vision you saw. And
then...you smile...promising yourself that even if the whole world is
against you, you would stand by your side. You might rest, or change
the route...but you would not change what you stand for.

❊ ❊ ❊

**You tell yourself "A dream might have gone sour but
not the eyes that saw it".**

284

**When was the last time you ate something,
forgetting everything else in the world…**

❋ ❋ ❋

… getting lost in its aroma…relishing its look…feeling its taste…just living it comprehensively? When I asked this question to the people of one of the growing food-chains of the city, all of them started sharing awkward glances…fidgeting and twitching in their chairs. Well, certainly not a great way to start a training session…or is it?

One of them said "We eat quickly so that we can get back to work", another said "I somehow steal time for it", yet another said "I almost feel guilty when I stop my work to go for lunch", and one ended up saying "there are many more important things waiting to be done".

❋ ❋ ❋

**Well, I've heard 'City never sleeps'.
Obviously it can't, unless it eats properly.**

285

**Have you wondered why when people die...
they suddenly become so special to us?**

* * *

Because now it is convenient to love them as they can't generate any more reasons to hate, it is convenient to talk about them as they can't intervene, it is convenient to speculate about them as they are not there to retaliate, and it is convenient to declare conclusions about them as they are no more a part of the analysis. Now...we own them, their persona is at the mercy of our imagination, we have all the control on who we want them to be to us.

While their life was a process, after death it becomes an event, and it is always more fun to narrate events than to describe processes. The truth is...it takes a lot of guts to love people the way they are, so we rather choose to love our versions of them. And when they are no more, there are no diversions...now we can love them on our own terms.

* * *

You see...it is all about us.

286

**Why only succeed, when we can
do a better thing?**

❋ ❋ ❋

Many of us live life as if it is a race and we have to reach somewhere…
beyond others…before others. And this tendency is born out of
one fixed-notion of success that the society had created in our
minds during our formative years. Society positioned 'success' as a
comparative term while in truth it is a standalone concept…and it is
everyone's birth-right to decide one's own definition for it.

Well, in English, 'Good' is a positive word, 'Better' its comparative
form and 'Best' its superlative. When we had not invented language,
life didn't have any positives, comparatives & superlatives; back
then 'Better' was not a word, it was a way of living. We didn't judge,
compare or certify, we simply tried more and different…Today, we
know it as Evolution.

❋ ❋ ❋

**Let's not just succeed.
Let's evolve.**

287

**Let's not wish all 'the best'
for ourselves.**

❋ ❋ ❋

Strange are the ways of the world! Why can't we appreciate what we don't have or can't get? When we find a beautiful rose then we say "I wish my balcony had it"…when we come across a swanky house then we say "One day, I would build such"…and when we see a pretty angelic face then we look at his/her partner and say "Damn Lucky Fellow"!

Whenever we see beauty in its highest glory then why can't we simply feel the bliss of witnessing its blossom… appreciate God's aesthetic sense…and experience the vicarious pleasure of being born in its life and times! Why can't we sometimes just admire things…without a desire to possess them!

❋ ❋ ❋

**Think about it when next time you say
"I got to get one like that"!**

288

**The longest running organized-conspiracy of society has been...
"caging woman in her own body".**

* * *

By writing poetry around her beauty, creating sculptures on her
gorgeousness and painting portraits of love for her, we have reduced
her to a set of vital-statistics with her self-esteem becoming directly
proportional to being an object of desire to someone else but herself.
As a result we have two kinds of woman...one who is in inferiority
complex of not fitting into the society's criteria of beauty, and another
who has confidence due to scoring high on them. Although she may
not realize it but in either case she is trapped.

In the first case, her mind is blocked in what she lacks, and in the
second, her mind is locked in what she has. And the result is same.
Now she doesn't have much mind-space left for her soul-searching...
or for enjoying what she actually enjoys. Well, if soul is God then
body is temple. So the body needs to be respected and restored but
not to be held in exaggerated importance over what it preserves. It
cannot forget that it is also a vehicle for the creators whose adobe it
is...the mind and soul.

* * *

**And what worse! If you observe carefully, the same 'body
conspiracy' is now getting extended to men.**

289

We hate critics not for their opinions, but for triggering our dormant insecurities.

* * *

The fact is that the most of what we feel, think, say or do is not our own. It is a result of years of social programming we have gone through. In other words - upbringing and education. So, need of approval is as basic a need as food, shelter or clothes. Now, suppose that I write something new. Now, actually I am myself not completely sure of how good it is (no one ever can be). Assume that now someone says it is good…then others also say so…then more…even more…and so on. With each nod, my confidence in being good grows…my self-image improves… I start enjoying it. So far, so good.

Imagine that now suddenly someone says "It's not good". Now, the moment he says it, the original doubt that I had in myself comes back to fore. As a result, now a conflict begins inside me, between my original doubting-self and my recently discovered confident-self. My first reaction will be to convince myself that I am still good so I will just ignore it. If more voices join the opposition then I'll become defensive. If equal number starts saying so then I'll turn aggressive. If majority starts agreeing then I will get depressed. And if everyone starts saying it then I will simply give up (my doubting-self has won).

* * *

Thus… the best way to deal with criticism is not by taking the criticism lightly… but by taking praise less seriously.

290

**Real relationships are
always 'tuned in' in an effortless manner.**

* * *

There is no pressure to prove, preserve or pamper. Whenever you stretch your hand…you find theirs. With such people, even a short conversation is fulfilling. And it isn't actually what they say but the shared-silence, when you are allowed a space to simply be. Those few moments when someone isn't there and…still is.

Well, at the heart of it, all human relations are about the same things…caring through words, supporting through actions… and at times… just 'being there', without a temptation to judge or hurry to conclude.

* * *

**We just need to figure out
when to choose which one.**

291

**When you help someone, remember that
gratitude can create immense awkwardness.**

❊ ❊ ❊

Somewhere inside, every person is self-centered and would always use every possible opportunity to raise his self-esteem. Now, when you extend a favor to someone then just observe his body-language – his shoulders drop, spine bows, neck bends, voice wavers, volume lessens, eyes look downwards… in all, his whole being gets shrunk.

In such moments, you may like him more but the truth is… he hates himself. And when someone hates himself in your presence then sooner or later he begins to hate you. So then, he either looks for the first chance to unburden himself by returning the favor, or takes a subconscious revenge by keeping exploiting you through flattery. And if neither is possible…he simply avoids you.

❊ ❊ ❊

**So when you help people, help them believe that
they succeeded because of themselves.**

292

**Only someone imperfect can be loved,
perfection only intimidates.**

* * *

People love you in a package-deal. They are as much in love with your
flaws as with your qualities. In fact, your flaws help them feel needed,
and also make them feel good about themselves (that they love you
in spite of them). So when they say "Why do you call my nick-name
in front of everyone?", "You forgot to call me!", "Why do you drive so
fast?", "Where did you keep the keys?", "Don't use that word again!",
"Again the same song!", "Why same color?", "How boring?" etc… then
they are actually falling more in love with you.

That's why, when you remove those flaws, then to them it only reads
as "you have changed"! And they simply don't like that (even if it
is for better). So don't you worry about those little niggles. They
make you imperfect…and thus…lovable. In a world where the head
cleverly maintains associations, the heart has reserved its rights on
relationships.

* * *

**And it is special, in the sense that
it doesn't try to change the one it loves.**

293

**In relationship, you can only bring
what you have.**

* * *

The biggest symptom of a pseudo-relationship is when "you want the person to be happy only with you…and if he is happy without you then you start feeling that he doesn't love you anymore". Well, relationships were meant for happiness but increasingly people are entering them for all the wrong reasons – to revive self-esteem, impress others, dispel loneliness or just for some fun.

As a result, what was meant to be a synergistic bliss ends up being an ugly battle for sadistic-pleasures; to be derived at the cost of each other's happiness. Well, those who enter relationship should remember that the most characteristically unique thing about happiness is that…

* * *

"You can't get it unless you give it".

294

**Second-hand solutions cannot solve
first-foot problems.**

❋ ❋ ❋

In the name of education, we are making people judgmental; passing on to them a narrow sense of right and wrong. In a controlled and structured environment, we pump idealism in them. But when they step out, there is a chaos out there – Queues are broken, rules are tossed, relations are far from perfect, truth doesn't always prevail and nice-guys may indeed finish last.

As a result, they start believing that world is wrong and they are right. They become critical or disillusioned. They waste a lot of energy, getting consumed in that state of denial; with utopian notions of justice and fairness that are far removed from reality-bites. So, let's allow people to create their own philosophies – not theoretical, but the empirical ones. But for that, first it is important to avoid talking about idealistic-views in a tone that makes them sound like laws. Rather they should be proposed as hypotheses to be verified, and people should be encouraged to stay skeptic until faith emerges inside them.

❋ ❋ ❋

**Education should empower…foster individuality.
It should create individuals – the life-ready people.**

295

We are not indispensable in anybody's life.

* * *

Now, there is a choice – we can either get disillusioned and cynical about this or can be appreciative of God's aesthetic sense for creating life with such an elegant flow. Latter is better because although it deprives us of our imagined-importance to everyone around us, it also relieves us of the pressure born out of such importance.

But there is an exception. We might be replaceable in everyone's life but once-gone we cannot come back in our own life. Yes, we have come in our life just for once…the first and last time. So, it's important (and preferable) to be self-centric (not self-centered) in life and derive a lot of happiness from within. After all, you got to be a source of happiness for being a resource for happiness.

* * *

Do remember…You aren't replaceable in your own life.

296

If something makes you happy today, then it has already become a potential source of sorrow for tomorrow.

* * *

If you have been happy after getting a person in your life then you would surely be miserable when the person would go away… if you have been happier after getting success then you would definitely turn out to be a grouchy loser… if your popularity makes you proud then your oblivion is going to be painful…

…If a possession made you feel heavenly then its loss will feel like the end of the world… if you are proud of your intelligence then any smarter guy will make you feel inferior… if your good-health is the cause of your pleasure then any sickness is enough to pull you down in the dumps. In life, every joy comes with a guarantee of sadness… it's just a matter of time – the warranty period.

* * *

Remember this truth even when you don't need to, so that, when you will face it, it'll hurt less.

297

Time is not money.

❋ ❋ ❋

In this era of consumerism, we have started treating our lives as some financial year where we have to produce quarterly results. With this 'time is money' belief, we evaluate everything in terms of ROI... even emotions. We want efficiency, even in relationships. However, let's remember that the only way to begin, enrich, strengthen or revive a relationship is to be together. No amount of justifications, gifts or facilities can compensate for the time. Yes, it is the biggest investment, sacrifice or payback that there is.

So apply your best will and discretion and steal whatever you can from the clutches of time and space...to create some moments of togetherness. Talk heart-to-heart... listen unconditionally... take a walk... stare sky from the terrace... go for a long drive... share a coffee... dine cozily or maybe, just sit alongside and experience the quietness of an evening. Go... Spend time, and be there.

❋ ❋ ❋

**...because the best gift you can ever bring
to those you love is...You.**

298

**To avoid is to leave 'a void'
inside your own self.**

* * *

There are many unwanted people in our life whom we have to
bear for various reasons – either we have inherited them, got them
by circumstantial choice-less-ness or who have come as part of a
package deal (they are important to the people who are important
to us). It is good to deal with them in an emotionally-neutral way –
behave normal… sound formal… talk general… discuss nominal…
and stay ignorantly negligent towards their irritant-talent.

It is so because trying to forget someone is a sure way to remember
them. When you avoid anyone then they start constraining your
choices and restricting your reach. Their existence gets magnified,
eclipsing your own. This repulsion towards them creates a tension
inside your own mind, blocking a chunk of your valuable mindshare.
So remember! When you avoid looking at the garbage, then your
house stinks more. Better see it and deal with it. And yes, shut-up
while you do it…or else you end up breathing even more stink.

* * *

**Thus, unless they are too abusive or unsafe-with…
take such people in your stride.**

299

**Money is a great motivator
but a bad motivation.**

❋ ❋ ❋

It is at best a byproduct of doing something for others, or better than others. So what matters is what brought it. It is not about enjoying money, but actually also enjoying the whole process of creating it. It is so because nothing corrupts a person like the money he does not deserve… and nothing corrodes a person like the money he has not enjoyed earning.

Yes, in extreme circumstances, money is extremely important but that's all its real utility is – in making you feel secure. It's when you start using it for making you feel good that the whole thing becomes a 'Big Bad trap'. The truth is…everyone dies with some money still left in their savings… so when you can never consume it all…then why let it consume you totally.

❋ ❋ ❋

**Well, in package tour, don't get obsessed with package…
in the end, it's about the tour.**

300

**I feel in life, we are too wordy
to be at-peace…**

❋ ❋ ❋

…talking a tad too much, keen on filling every pause with any sound and trying to express everything and impress everyone. On the other hand, silence is beautiful. Look around! Most of the beautiful things around us are silent –the meditative Buddha, dancing trees, starry sky, serene lake, fragrant flowers or a sleeping baby. All melting effortlessly into their background…all so complete in themselves – arrived; pure existence; no strings attached.

Yes, silence is enriching. Relationships gain their depth during the moments of shared silences…when you are neither dependent on each other nor independent of each other…but simply coexisting. No motive to persuade, no agenda to dominate, no desperation to dodge voids and no aspiration to create joy… just being there. Silence is revitalizing –when we speak, we move outward…and when we are silent, we turn inward… discovering the treasure within – the scope of observation, the seed of realization, the source of creativity and the origin of happiness.

❋ ❋ ❋

**Well, one evolution happened when man invented language.
Another is due when…he will reinvent silence.**

301

Permanents shouldn't be based on temporaries.

* * *

There are times when because of necessity or proximity, you spend a lot of time with someone. And as a result, you develop certain shared-space. This predictability is assuring… this habit of someone is really comforting. There are times when someone fills a void in your life – void born out of low self-esteem or loneliness. And when that person caters to your need of feeling good about yourself you start enjoying that high…that importance. And then there are times when you like a person – either get infatuated with looks, impressed with intellect, attracted to presence or awed by worldly belongings. And if it is reciprocated, the whole feeling of a prized possession makes you feel exclusive.

But all these are reasons too fragile to found a lasting commitment on. Well, beyond a person's assets, appeal and attitudes lay a person's fundamental self – the basic nature. Dig for it, and see if you find it worth living with…because eventually that's what you end up living with. For committed relationships, don't choose a person who is good towards you…rather choose a person who is good towards most; because former is good by choice and latter is good by 'nature'.

* * *

**Do remember, eventually,
we all revert to our nature.**

302

Suffering comes in all shapes and sizes.

✳ ✳ ✳

I have seen people suffering loss of their parents, and then have also seen the ones whose parents are causing them huge emotional-trauma. I have seen people missing that they never had siblings and also the ones who wished they actually never had one. I have seen people suffering because they couldn't get the ones they loved, and also the ones who got them but are now suffering equally in their very hands.

That's why I don't understand why people compare their sufferings. After all, pain is such an individual concept…so personal in nature that it can never be measured for two persons on one common continuum; and then benchmarked or put side by side. It comes in all shapes and sizes. It is so 'irrationally private' that you just cannot understand, estimate or juxtapose.

✳ ✳ ✳

**Pain is a standalone concept,
don't see it in a networked setup.**

303

**Authenticity isn't an apparent concept,
it has to be scanned for.**

* * *

Over the years, I have seen so many people who care genuinely, get things done and push for better; yet are often interpreted to be bad just because they lose balance. Then there are people who just get along, pass by and hang around; and are still interpreted as good because they don't lose it.

World of humans operates at a superficial level. We have a clear preference for behavior over attitude. That's why a nice word passes off as a good deed. Sadly, in a society where managing perceptions has become more important than intentions and image has outplayed substance, we have made it difficult for genuineness to survive. And then we complain about the shortage.

* * *

**Scratch the surface, or you may end up counting
on pebbles…and losing out on gems.**

304

Sharp memory isn't good for happiness.

* * *

The best thing about past is that there is a certainty about it…it is safe…known territory…within our control. And it also gives a facility to pick and choose…to ignore what we find unnecessary, focus on what serves our purpose and change interpretations to suit our liking. Well, the backyard belongs to us, that's why we like it there.

But real-life doesn't have a reverse gear. Past is only virtual. Find it somewhere and you will find it nowhere. The cosmos didn't even take pains to erase it, it simply got overwritten. All incidents and events now only remain in your mind and it's you who refuse to truncate the recycle-bin. Well, life's favorite button is F5. So, all you can do is 'Redo'…

* * *

… but for that, you have to first stop wasting time in finding the 'Undo' feature in the 'Help' menu.

305

Life is a stream…and has a natural flow to it.

* * *

Problem starts when we try to resist the flow - when we repeatedly call someone who has moved on… when we keep texting to those who have deleted our contact-details… when we convince people to stay when they don't want to be there anymore … when we keep looking at facebook-accounts of people who have already gone past us.

Well, don't push it hard. If it's not coming naturally then it only means that it doesn't have a role in the grand plan now. Don't question the relevance of what you can't understand…trust that beyond reason lies a higher force called 'Destiny'…taking us towards our 'Destinations'.

* * *

And Yes, focus on those who the flow has now brought into your life…equally unreasonably.

306

It's not over, so why overreact?

❉ ❉ ❉

There are phases in life when you are not at the top of your game. Startled by the realization of how fragile your infallibility is, you feel down and the demons of self-doubt come back to feed on your confidence. In response to this sudden attack, your ego stands up to fight for itself. You sulk, crib, isolate yourself or tend to spill it out at anything that can take the beating.

Well, such days are a gentle reminder for you to rediscover the humbleness you had when you started out…much before you acquired an image, and all the miscellaneous attached to it. So, when things are getting on your nerves and you are barely getting along, then don't get back at life…get back to yourself. See it through, and wait for the tide to turn…which it will – sooner or later.

❉ ❉ ❉

**It's a part of the game…and
you got to take it in your stride.**

307

Happiness doesn't lie in attainment, it's in rationalization or anticipation.

* * *

I would wonder why people don't want to face reality and rather build their cocoons and spend life inside them…avoiding questions and dreading answers. As I began working with and on people, I figured out why! It is because…"they want to be happy". Well, happiness has nothing to do with what you have. It is not about reality…it is notional.

It is about 'perceptions about present' and 'assumptions about future'. So, you have to either believe that all is fine or…that it will be. You have to have an ignorant faith: that you are good or you will soon be; you are successful or will soon become; someone likes you or soon would; someone understands you or soon will; in all…you are happy or soon shall be. And when you analyze, the ignorance bids you bye, and…so does the faith.

* * *

And you become an unhappy intellectual.

308

Taking decision is a lonely job.

* * *

It suddenly reminds you of how standalone you are in a seemingly networked world. What makes it worse is that the moment you take a decision; it solicits a series of unattractive to-dos and attracts a series of unsolicited consequences. And if you are the one who put his foot down then they all come on your head.

So the best decision people take is…not to take one. Well, but they forget that the loneliness of taking a decision and the burden of bearing what comes in the wake of it is the only way to initiate, create, contribute, and above-all…build that all-important sense of 'Self' that helps us evolve.

* * *

Make the decision …because then… it'll make you.

309

**"There will always be someone who won't like you".
So get comfortable with the idea of being disliked.**

* * *

'Positive' and 'negative' always coexist. In fact, they can be identified only relative to each other. So, to be happy, you have to accept the polarity and train yourself to focus more on the former. Be with people who like to be with you and don't chase the elusive idea of converting someone disinterested into 'yours'. Even if you are able to, the maintenance cost will be far too high.

Focus not on being liked but on what makes you likeable. And then don't sell around, just represent what you have and leave it on others to decide if that's what they value. And if they hurl negatives on you then sympathize, as one can only give what one has. Well, and if you still can't avoid negative people, then minimize their intervention. Keep them at bare minimum – if not in your routine, then at least in your thoughts.

* * *

**Yes, don't wish thorns away…just
see through them.**

310

**See people how they are...not how
you wish they were.**

* * *

Well, if you are sensitive then it is a gem that God has gifted you with. Now, you have to cherish it, safeguard it and not let it become your concern. This is only possible when you don't fool yourself into looking at people the way you want them to be, but see them the way they are. Observe people carefully, and when you discover something about them that you don't like then don't feel irritated, disappointed or panicky. When they hurt you then see them objectively, as they reveal their hidden agendas, ulterior motives and...their true selves.

When you do so, you would see the games people play – culprits posing as victims, connivance in the veil of helplessness, the contempt in the niceness, the deal beneath the help, in short...minds behind the faces. Don't be a skeptic but nor miss the subtle cues. Well, most importantly, see them, not to be cynical or to lose faith in goodness; but to be able to select the worthy those who really deserve the gold of your heart.

* * *

**If you're sensitive, don't regret or change...
just be more observant & slightly selective.**

311

**In life, playing multiple roles progressively
is the key to relationship-success.**

❋ ❋ ❋

When two persons start a relationship, they start as lover and beloved. All is well, because that's the only role one expects the other one to play. However, as they formalize their bonding into an arrangement, many other roles get added to the expectation-list. And that's when…things start changing.

So, then you have a case where someone succeeds as a beloved, fails as a life-partner, excels as a provider but just about gets by as a family-builder. Yes, the same person, doing differently in different roles expected of him or her. And now, that person looks good or a let-down to you depending on the role which is at the top of your expectation-list at a certain point of time.

❋ ❋ ❋

**Yes, people start out as persons and…
end up being role-players.**

312

**You might feel pleasure on extremes, but
the happiness can only be found in balance.**

❊ ❊ ❊

People yearn for peaks, the moments of thrill on the thresholds – the proverbial 'living on the edge'. That rush of blood through the veins giving a 'high' unparalleled, making you feel alive – pulsating and throbbing. It is exhilarating, addictive and a dose of pure delight. That's why people buy brands, drive fast, party hard, dance dirty, puff pricey and drink bottoms-up. They just want to 'live it up'.

But the problem with pleasure is that you always seek that feeling which you had for the 'first' time; and it only lasts till the last time you had it. Yes, it just doesn't add-up. And the result is a generation of people running fast and furiously on a treadmill, only to realize later that they haven't gone any further. Well, it is good to be 'young and restless' for a while, but the problem is that when you rest less, you don't remain young for long.

❊ ❊ ❊

Yes, in the long run…'mileage matters'.

313

**Every pain is pregnant with a transformation,
don't behave like the patient, act like the gynecologist.**

* * *

The other day, someone asked me *"Why is it that whenever I go through difficult times, no one is there for me…they all turn their backs?"* I said *"…so that it can officially be termed 'difficult times'"*. Yes, if in your difficult times, all people will stand by you, then how would it be difficult times? Their presence will never let you feel the severity of those times.

And every 'difficult times' is destiny's ploy to make you learn something that it deems shall be valuable for you. It might be an opportunity to evolve, develop patience, introspect, retrospect, reorient, or simply for realization of our eventual 'utter loneliness'. Well, but all people do is waste energy on feeling bad and holding grudges against those who turned their backs.

* * *

It is akin to 'criticizing a sign-board's design rather than seeing what it is indicating towards'.

314

We witness most of our life in our 'minds', imagined.

❋ ❋ ❋

In fact very little is happening outside. All of us are actually living our lives in our heads, affected more by the perceptions of events than the events themselves. If it was not the case then why would we sweat profusely and wake up panting after a bad dream. It felt so real while it lasted. Didn't it? So, beyond the circumstances you are in, how you feel about life is more a function of what you think.

And thus, every night when you go to sleep, you have to pick the points from the day that can be the reasons for you to be happy. It is your own responsibility to do this exercise because the decision to be happy or sad is solely taken inside one's head, removed from and irrespective of what has actually happened during the course of the day. Every day, we all create our own little heavens and hells, and then take a customized tour for free.

❋ ❋ ❋

And well, if it is free, why let it cost you your happiness?

315

**Every player should remember that
they play best when there is 'total immersion'.**

* * *

Some people pre-play everything. They keep thinking about what they will do, and then what will happen, and then what will they do when that will happen. As a result, all prospective positive things lose charm when they eventually take place. It is because, no matter how positive it is, it's very hard for any reality to compete with an imagined version of reality. Thus, their happiness always falls short of their idea of happiness.

And then some people replay everything. They keep thinking about what had happened, and with every subsequent replaying they subconsciously keep sprinkling some or other new topping to it. And they don't even realize that, with time, what they eventually remember is not the original memory but their remix of it, with everything changed except the key notes. And slowly, rather than enjoying 'the moment', they begin to enjoy 'thinking about it later'. Well, in either case, one cannot achieve true happiness…as…

* * *

…True happiness doesn't lie in pre-playing or replaying the moment. It lies in simply playing…with the momentum.

316

**You cannot create what you don't get attached to…
and you cannot enjoy what you get too attached to.**

** * **

There are two kinds of people. First are 'the minimizers' – they live on the surface. For them, everything is a task. Be it in relationships or at work, they maintain objectivity. They don't relate to things, they simply get connected to them. They go through the motion, without immersing themselves in the act or the purpose. They simply plug-in and plug-out. But alas, they seldom create anything…they pass through life 'mostly successfully', but without fulfillment or significance.

And then there are 'maximizers'. They get deeply involved. They don't just participate, they lose themselves in the act. They can't 'eject', and thus keep going through the highs and lows. They are often heartbroken, exhausted or weighed down by their own expectations. They attach their self-worth to what they relate to, and so it keeps dwindling. But alas, they neither experience the joy of the journey nor enjoy the feel of the destination.

** * **

Let's be optimizers…the ones who get attached, but never too attached… the ones who get detached, but never too detached.

317

**Many couples start out as soul-mates and eventually
end up becoming more like… room-mates.**

＊ ＊ ＊

At the start, every relationship seems to possess a spark that is hard
to define…some sort of a 'magic'. However, if you look closely, that
magic is combination of two factors – the 'connection' that the
two persons share, and the unique set of 'circumstances' they find
themselves in. Now, naturally, the circumstances change over a period
of time, and thus then onward the relationship heavily depends on
the 'connection' between the two persons.

Sadly, this connection is hard to retain, and even harder to regain
if lost. And without that connection, persons get pulled apart, and
the 'strain' is palpable. However, it is worth every effort to regain
that connect, because that's what provides the most important
nourishment for a fulfilling life. And the good news is that the
ingredients which are needed to regain that connect are quite simple
– spending time with each other, giving undivided attention, seeing
each other's positives, bringing back the innocence to trust each
other, and showing care and concern. Yup! That's all it takes.

＊ ＊ ＊

**But here comes the bad news… "As people grow up, they become
so complex that for them, doing simple things is no more easy".**

318

**No one thinks about you as much as
you think they do.**

❊ ❊ ❊

To most of the people out there, you are at best a fleeting thought in the mind which too comes only when either something related to you is 'trending' in their lives, or if something related to you incidentally pops up in their attention arena. And even those who you think are obsessed with you – any new relationship, or an old relationship with new major developments – think about you a lot at stretch, but only in patches.

They also keep toggling their attention between you and other usual or pressing matters. So effectively, total span of your intrusion in their minds is also only marginal. So, in all… Sorry dude! Irrespective of what you think of yourself, you don't matter that much to anyone out there. That should be disheartening…isn't it? Actually…not quite.

❊ ❊ ❊

That should rather be liberating.